AF291998

Colditz: The Escapes

Colditz: The Escapes

Peter Hawthorne

Pen & Sword
MILITARY

First published in Great Britain in 2026 by
Pen & Sword Military
An imprint of Pen & Sword Books Limited
Yorkshire – Philadelphia

ISBN 978 1 03614 886 7

Typeset by Mac Style
Printed in the UK by CPI Group (UK) Ltd, Croydon, CR0 4YY.

The Publisher's authorised representative in the EU for product
safety is Authorised Rep Compliance Ltd., Ground Floor,
71 Lower Baggot Street, Dublin D02 P593, Ireland.
www.arccompliance.com

For a complete list of Pen & Sword titles please contact:

PEN & SWORD BOOKS LIMITED
47 Church Street, Barnsley, South Yorkshire, S70 2AS, England
E-mail: enquiries@pen-and-sword.co.uk
Website: www.pen-and-sword.co.uk
or
PEN AND SWORD BOOKS
1950 Lawrence Road, Havertown, PA 19083, USA
E-mail: uspen-and-sword@casematepublishers.com
Website: www.penandswordbooks.com

For Emma, Autumn and Elowyn.
My world.

Contents

List of Plates

Acknowledgements

In 2012 I was fortunate enough to rely on some excellent advice and editorial skills from friends and family when my first book, *The Animal Victoria Cross*, was published. In 2025 I have been just as fortunate. My wife has been a constant of unwavering support and the editors-in-chief, my daughters, have provided some particularly strong feedback as I read the stories to them at bedtime. If the account was well written and held their attention, they would be kind enough to say that the story was 'good'; however, if I glanced up from the page to hear a gentle snore, I knew I needed to revisit the version I had written. More subtle advice on this book came from my mother, Ann Hawthorne, who diligently read through draft after draft, and my neighbours, Paul and Linda Bennett and Sharon and Kev Whitehouse, have studied each tale of escape and supported with helpful advice on the pace of language. My Godmother, Jackie Smith, read the final draft before it was sent to Pen and Sword and provided kind words which every budding writer needs before dispatching a draft. Dr Laurie Davis provided valuable knowledge and expertise on the repatriation escapes with detailed explanations of the symptoms and an understanding of the standard of German medical knowledge of the period.

The research for this book has taken many years and I relied heavily on Pat Reid's *Colditz* to fire my interest in the Castle itself and the daring tales of escape. The BBC production in the early 1970s also drove my imagination of what it must have been to stand in the shoes of men who dared to escape an Oflag which Reich Marshal Hermann Göring boasted was escape-proof. As I read through the lengths each man embraced in order to facilitate the merest hope of an escape, I wanted to write a book on the thirty-two prisoners who managed the remarkable achievement of a 'home run'. At Pen and Sword the excellent production assistant Harriet Fielding put up with my emails and requests for advice on what to include and what to omit, her patience and support was invaluable in the last few months. Research and writing a book may take many years and months, but the last few weeks can make all the difference and Harriet's support and knowledge were vital, and this book is all the better for her guidance. Andrew Webb at the Imperial War Museum was also extremely supportive, spending long hours researching photographs from Colditz during the war years. Mrs Maria Binfield was very helpful with translations of documents from German to English and the diligent work of Stephen Chumbley ensured this book was thoroughly prepared for publication.

My final acknowledgement is to you, the reader, I wished to convey how the prisoners felt at the moment they jumped the fence or snipped the wire. The book hopes to give you the feeling of excitement and danger each man experienced as they fled the Castle, and euphoria when they achieved their home run. Finally, I hope you enjoy reading this book as much as I enjoyed writing it.

Best wishes
Peter Hawthorne
March 2025

Introduction –
What qualifies as a legitimate escape?

Colditz Castle was originally built in 1014 as a huge and resplendent hunting lodge for the kings of Saxony. In its thousand-year history it has been the setting for battles, sieges and became a royal hunting lodge for the nobility. During the Hussite wars of the early fifteenth century it was nearly destroyed, only to be extensively rebuilt as a wedding present to the Danish princess who wed the Elector of Saxony. Further damage was caused when a bakery servant named Clemens Bock burned down the town in 1504. Frederick the Wise rebuilt Colditz Castle from 1506 in a Renaissance style with additional space for royalty and fine art and decoration. Renovation of the Castle was completed by Sophia of Brandenburg from 1603 who developed gardens around the Castle including ponds, grottos and a vineyard. Shortly afterwards war rested on the steps of the Castle once more. Colditz, as a Protestant town, came under heavy siege in the Thirty Years war. Eventually Swedish troops hostile to Catholicism recaptured the Castle and held their ground. In 1706, during the Battle of Fraustadt, the Castle witnessed a remarkable victory for Swedish troops, who with just 8,000 men and no artillery defeated a Russian force twice their size. Colditz received little damage in this period and soon returned to become a home for the Dukes of Saxony. From 1800 the Castle became a workhouse for beggars and tramps and in 1829 it became a State Institute for the Mentally Ill.

The Nationalist Socialist government led by Adolf Hiter requisitioned Colditz Castle as a prison camp for political opponents and 'displaced persons'. By late 1939 the German Blitzkrieg offensive had swept up a number of prisoners of war which were housed in forts and purpose-built camps with a barbed wire perimeter fence. To the committed escape artist this was an initiation test, and many officers made light work of regaining their freedom, although finding safe passage to neutral Switzerland or a ship prepared to transport them to the United Kingdom was difficult and recapture was often the outcome. Gradually Allied officers became such persistent planners of escape that the German High Command required an escape-proof prison, deep in Eastern Germany. Colditz Castle provided such a place. Built high up on a rocky outcrop with the River Zwickauer Mulde flowing nearby as a medieval defence, the Castle had tall imposing walls and a small town of residents who were committed to the Reich.

On 7 November 1940 the first British contingent arrived to join the Polish men who were already stationed at the camp, known as Oflag IV-C. Gradually more Allied officers arrived including Belgians, French and Dutch who were all branded as 'troublesome or persistent escape artists'. The inmates also included *Prominente* who were political prisoners such as Giles Romilly, the nephew of Winston Churchill. Over the next four years there were 183 recorded escape attempts. The security officer at Colditz, Reinhold Eggers, established a museum in the Castle with exhibits, disguises and forged identity papers to educate his guards and prevent further escapes.

In recent years there has been considerable historical debate as to what exactly constitutes a successful escape from Colditz. These men were amongst the bravest to serve in the Second World War and risked everything to ensure maximum disruption to the German war machine. Vital resources were diverted to guarding these men and the effort, time and money required to track down the men who escaped harmed the war effort of Nazi Germany. There were over 180 escapes from early 1941 to the autumn of 1944. The Poles were amongst the first prisoners to be incarcerated at Colditz, with the Laufen Six, including Major Pat Reid, shortly afterwards. Soon Belgians, Dutch and French made up a community of committed officers hell-bent on escape with a wide variety of skills to exchange and hone, there was also an escape by the Indian national, Dr Biren Mazumdar.

Discussion over whether an escape can be considered legitimate if it is from beyond the Castle walls is a thorny issue. The castle includes the exercise yard which was always heavily guarded. If a prisoner engineered his movement or escape from the Castle or devised an outright escape is acceptable. Many prisoners went to local train stations for 'medical reasons', or were escorted into the town of Colditz to see the dentist or to be placed in the town jail when solitary confinement inside Colditz was full. Some men actively engaged in 'goon-baiting' (antagonizing the guards) so as to obtain a court martial, which would be held in a court away from the Castle, a dangerous game to play if the prisoner did not escape before his court appearance. Ordinary Germans whose existence was in peril by RAF bombing raids and food shortages were often keen to make an example of disobedient prisoners of war with the sentences they handed down.

The criteria for a successful escape or 'home run' is that the prisoner must have been a permanent prisoner within the camp, and should have escaped from the Castle under his own steam or engineered his way out of the Castle (to be treated in a hospital for a real or faked illness or to a court martial). For this reason, the escape of Lieutenant van Lynden has not been included. As an officer of the Netherlands, he escaped from Colditz courtesy of all prisoners of Dutch nationality being moved to a different camp in Stanislau. Taking his opportunity on the march, van Lynden slipped away undetected and reached neutral territory. In addition, the escape of French Lieutenant Raymond Bouillez is also not included. Bouillez was sent to Colditz to await trial in Stuttgart and was not a formal prisoner of the Castle. After a short stay he was en route to his court martial when he jumped from the moving train and sustained serious injuries. Whilst convalescing in a military hospital he regained enough strength to disappear and travel home to Vichy France.

The destination of a prisoner's escape is just as contentious: is neutral territory a home run? Or simply a safe house within occupied territory, or is it only a successful escape if the prisoner returns to the United Kingdom or the country of their birth? To answer these questions any home run would include a prisoner reaching neutral territory and a safe house on one of the 'Ratlines' (routes of safe passage across Europe) which ferried men from Switzerland toward Gibraltar and ships which enabled many to reach the United Kingdom. For this reason the escape of Lieutenant William Anderson Millar is included in the thirty-two listed in this book. Millar was killed in action as a result of a decision taken on 2 March 1944 when Heinrich Himmler authorized a document known as 'Aktion K', translated as Action Kugel (Bullet). Millar reached a safe house in Czechoslovakia but was intercepted and subsequently shot at Mauthausen.

Finally, the escape known as 'working their ticket' was a method of liberation which involved a prisoner faking illness to achieve repatriation. This was a very challenging method of escape, as the prisoner had to convince the German doctors within the camp. But due to shortages of staff there was often no trained clinician on duty and frequently a vet was the best option. The Medical Commission was also prohibited from entering the Castle, which meant that a prisoner had to keep up the pretence of illness for years. It was only in 1944 that the Medical Commission entered the Castle and a list of twenty-nine men was put forward for repatriation: of this list five are considered to have 'worked their ticket'. For some this was the culmination of years of acting. In some cases prisoners deliberately worsened their condition to convince their German captors and Commission doctors of their suitability for inclusion on the list.

This leaves us with just thirty-three successful escapes from the 'escape-proof' Colditz Castle. Contained in this book are the accounts of how each man managed to escape.

British Escapes

Squadron Leader Brian Paddon – Great Britain

Born on 24 August 1908 in Carshalton, Surrey, Brian Paddon was the son of the Reverend Charles Salmon Paddon, and spent his childhood in the village of Lannarth, Cornwall. Paddon joined the RAF in June 1929 and obtained his Royal Aero Club Aviation licence in September 1932. Upon the outbreak of war he was deployed in the Battle of France in 1939–40 and engaged the enemy frequently over the winter months. Whilst flying his Bristol Blenheim on 6 June 1940 he was shot down during the attack on Saint Valery-en-Caux and was captured.

After interrogation he was dispatched, briefly, to Spangenberg before acting as the Senior British Officer at Stalag Luft I at Barth. Paddon was given the nickname 'Never a Dull Moment' and although it is unclear when he gained this moniker, his work at Stalag Luft I is characteristic of such a description. Paddon set about 'goon-baiting' and seizing every opportunity to escape from captivity. The German guards sent Paddon to Colditz and 'Never a Dull Moment' arrived on 14 May 1941 at the height of 'escape season'. On 22 June Paddon and fellow British officers had finished an exercise period and as they walked back toward the Castle they saw a young German woman walking along the path to the German courtyard. For many this was the first woman they had seen in over a year and some expressed appreciation with a chorus of whistles and catcalls, except Squadron Leader Paddon who noticed that her watch had slipped from her wrist and landed on the cobbled path. Immediately he collected the watch and set off after the lady who began to move quicker. The German guards took interest as the British officers cheered Paddon on as he closed in on the woman until with horror Paddon realized this was no German woman but Lieutenant

Boule, a French officer. Over many months Boule's wife had sent him items of her clothing including make-up and a long blonde wig so he could don the disguise and sneak out of the Castle. Poor Paddon had unwittingly exposed him by returning the watch and Boule was led away by the guards.

The detail the German guards and station masters searched for is illustrated by the precise way in which they studied the forged passes, as previous escapes floundered as it was recognized that fellow escapees had passes issued in different cities, but with the same handwriting

Paddon devoted so much time to escaping that his nickname was well deserved and during an escape prior to Colditz he left the military hospital at Gnaschwitz, but was quickly recaptured at a train station with his companion Josef Just. Just was an eccentric Pole who was searched alongside Paddon and the incrimination began when the latter's suitcase was found to contain a small saw and a wrench for disabling iron bars. It became significantly worse when Just was strip-searched and a number of clothing articles labelled 'Lt Just Oflag IV-C' were found. Needless to say, the escape was short-lived.

However, Paddon learned fast and made detailed notes, learning from each experience. The full list of 'Paddon Rules' comprised:

1. Travel on slow trains, there are no passes requested.
2. Express trains – between Leipzig and Dresden the Sergeant on checks requires only identity cards.
3. Passes can be recognized as forged by the police because of the following; – No such thing as a Branch Works Stamp (Nebenbauamt). – The signatures on Lt Just's card and mine were in the same handwriting – but different names. – The stamp was poor. – No such thing as a Bauinspektor (Building inspector). – Same handwriting on different passes, one issued in Dresden, one in Leipzig.
4. Brown pass ok for identification, not for travelling.
5. Best of all is a Leave Pass. Everyone asks for it and it comes with travel reductions. This is the key to everything and it must be a pleasure to travel with a good one.
6. Tuttlinggen is a frontier zone. Tickets to Stuttgart are issued sometimes with or without Identity cards being requested.
7. German civvies are of a better quality than expected, especially on a Sunday – therefore a bad day to travel.

8. It is always possible to get something to eat without coupons. Never again shall I carry Red Cross chocolate.
9. Remove all names and tags from clothes. Including Oflag IVC
10. He who travels best, travels alone.

During a search of the British quarters the Security Officer Reinhold Eggers discovered his escape notes and handed them to Kommandant Schmidt. Eggers was a shrewd choice by the Nazi High Command to oversee security at Colditz as Duty Officer and later Security Officer. A former schoolmaster, he spoke excellent English and had fought in the trenches during the First World War, winning an Iron Cross for bravery on the Somme. As a teacher he was acutely aware that placing all the naughty boys in one place might seem like a good idea, if the Castle was indeed escape proof, but the reality was that these prisoners would soon start learning from each other. Furthermore, they were not schoolchildren but men with considerable talents which they began to exchange and master. In the 1970s *Colditz* series produced by the BBC Bernard Hepton played the part of the Kommandant and commented that the Poles could open doors in the Castle than he could not even if he had the key! Later Eggers would discover that the expert lock pickers were Lieutenant Surmnowicz, Lieutenant 'Scarlett' O'Hara, Lieutenant Guiges and the Dutch officer Captain van Dooninck, one each from the nationalities who had students in each mess. Colditz was becoming a university for would-be escapers.

The opportunity for Paddon to utilize his rules for escaping came soon after his last failed attempt, He was summoned for court martial at Thorn (his previous camp) for insulting a sergeant major and accusing him of theft. Paddon's reputation meant that he was searched several times before leaving the Castle and was also X-rayed, but none of this resulted in the discovery of his cigar case 'arse-creeper' (used to hide money and placed in the rectum to avoid detection). The civilian clothes he had been given for his court appearance ensured he was prepared for his escape. Corporal Schadlich (or Pinkerton as Paddon had christened him) escorted Paddon to a camp at Thorn on a Sunday, Schadlich remained at the camp for the court martial and when they arrived he described Paddon as a '*sehr gefahrlicher Aubsbrecher*', a 'very dangerous breaker-out'. Immediately an opportunity presented itself to live up to his new billing. Paddon noticed lightly-guarded work parties would leave the camp each day, and the atmosphere was much more convivial than at Colditz. A sign on of the doors read 'In future British prisoners are not to be treated as criminals but POWs and a more friendly attitude must be observed toward them'. The court martial was due to start at 9.00 am, but the work parties left at 7.00 am which would give him two hours to join the party, slip away and get to a train station before the alarm would be raised. Paddon worked quickly to procure anything to aid his escape. He was given an oversized dirty battledress to smuggle himself into the work party, a thin Mappe briefcase and some rations. As Schadlich would no doubt inform the guards that prisoners from Colditz habitually made for Switzerland, the search would focus on the woods to the south. Paddon shrewdly decided to go north to Danzig. As a port the city had obvious attraction for an escaped prisoner of war looking for a ship to neutral territory, but Paddon had been given the address of a Polish officer's girlfriend from Thorn as well as a detailed handwritten map of the port from a Polish merchant seaman.

Just before 7.00 am the following morning Paddon joined the work party in his oversized and shabby battledress and was led to a field where the prisoners began work. For an experienced officer familiar with methods of escape it was easy to slip behind a large haystack undetected and change into blue RAF trousers, brown golf windcheater and peaked engine driver's hat, picking up the slim briefcase he set of on his bid for freedom. Boarding a train he travelled under the identity of Phillippe de Raeymakers, a Belgian worker, and slept in railway station waiting rooms confident that his German linguistic skills and identity papers would pass any scrutiny. Arriving safely in Danzig the plan was to wait until dark and smuggle aboard a ship bound for neutral waters, reveal himself to the crew and captain and ask for safe passage to the Swedish coast. So comfortable was Paddon that he happily engaged in conversation with others leaving the train and even caught a bus to the portside, making a point of helping an old lady down the steps to the curb. *Scharnhorst*, the impressive German battleship, was anchored in the harbour as Paddon passed the day at a pub drinking beer and chatting with sailors whilst watching the ships carefully. Darkness fell which provided cover for Paddon as he earmarked a Swedish merchant ship some 500 yards from a German sentry. Silently he slipped aboard and smuggled himself into the coal store submerging himself in a 'shallow grave'. Desperately bad luck struck as the Swedish vessel had not yet unloaded its cargo of iron ore and remained in Danzig harbour for three days and nights before finally moving from the Baltic Sea. Each night Paddon would creep up to the boiler and refill his water bottle.

Eventually Paddon decided to reveal himself on the bridge, covered in soot from head to toe, divulging his true name and identity and explaining that he requested safe passage to Sweden. It was not a warm welcome. The Swedish captain was angry: he demanded to know why Paddon had not waited until the ship had actually reached Sweden before announcing himself and thereby incriminating his ship and crew. In addition, another ship had arrived in Stockholm with a cargo of stowaways and the German authorities refused the vessel permission to coal in Danzig. The captain issued instructions for the ship to return to the coast and Paddon to be handed over to the nearest German sentry. Desperately, Paddon pleaded with him, appealing to international law, bribery and even to have the registration of the ship declared void with Lloyd's of London after the war; all to no avail. Finally, Paddon explained that his life would be at stake if the ship maintained its course for Danzig. The captain went below deck without an answer, leaving Paddon desperately concerned as he stared from the bridge waiting for Danzig to reappear. 'Do you speak Polish'. Paddon turned around and the Captain stood before him, with his second mate, Paddon mumbled enough Polish he had picked up in various camps unsure of what exactly it meant. It was good enough. 'You will present yourself as a Polish refugee in Gevle and remain in prison until we leave the port, understand?' Squadron Leader Brian Paddon became Stanislaw Rawinski.

Two Swedish policemen came aboard and promptly took Rawinski to the town jail where he was informed that once records have been taken he would, as a civilian refugee, have to return to the vessel and become a refugee in the final destination port of that particular journey. That was Hamburg! The thought of re-entering Germany as Stanislaw Rawinski carrying papers which said Phillippe de Raeymakers when he was actually Squadron Leader Brian Paddon, Colditz prisoner on the run, did not fill him with joy. In fact, he reasoned he would be lucky to avoid execution. Immediately he confessed to the Swedish police, explaining his story and his identities. Fortunately, the police decided to speak with the British consul who accepted his story and after a detailed interrogation, decided that Paddon should be flown to Scotland. Brian Paddon was only the fourth British officer to escape from the whole of Germany. Once he arrived in London he was given an audience at Buckingham Palace as the most senior British officer to escape at that point. Prisoners in Colditz were unaware of his escape, many believed he may have been executed. However, the Senior British Officer Daddy Stayner pressed the guards for an answer. Paddon had indeed completed a 'home run'.

Lieutenant Micky Wynn – United Kingdom

Robert Charles Michael Vaughan Wynn, the 7th Baron Newborough, was born on 24 April 1917 and became affectionately known as 'Micky Wynn'. Educated at Oundle School, he was commissioned into the 9th Lancers in 1935 before joining the 5th Royal Inniskilling Dragoon Guards and saw action at the outbreak of the Second World War. Sadly, due to injuries sustained in battle, Wynn was invalided out of the British Army in 1940. However, in May of that year British troops were desperate for sea rescue at Dunkirk and Wynn, now acting as a civilian, was given command of a yacht which acted as an air-sea rescue boat stationed out of Lee-on-Solent. Wynn made five successful trips to Dunkirk, rescuing many men, but on the last journey he was close to Ramsgate when shell fire damaged the ship beyond repair. Unperturbed, he volunteered to captain a Norfolk fishing boat and, dressed in full naval uniform in case he was arrested as a spy, set off for the beaches south of Calais, where he was told he would find soldiers sheltering in the sand dunes. Wynn returned without finding any further troops but the Royal Navy recognized his abilities and rewarded him with a commission in the Royal Navy Volunteer Reserve in July 1941.

Always eager to get into the fray, he became involved in designing depth charges which could be fired from a motor torpedo boat. The targets were the mighty battleships *Scharnhorst* and *Gneisenau*. Unfortunately while this experiment was still at trial stage both ships made a daring escape from Brest. However, all was not wasted. Further tests were carried out prior to the forthcoming raid on St Nazaire and adjustments made to the delayed-action mechanism of the torpedoes which were fired by *MTB 74* with such devastating effect.

Intelligence gathered by the Royal Navy indicated that the German battleship *Tirpitz* with its lethal 15in guns could only fit into one dry dock in Western Europe, the Louis Joubert dock in St Nazaire, Normandy. The decision was taken that this dry dock must be destroyed by a flotilla of vessels, armed with explosives, which would drift into the estuary and approach the target and rest next to the dry dock: detonation would occur through a timer. Operation Chariot was an audacious plan in which an ex-American destroyer *Campbeltown*, laden with twenty-four time-fused charges, was to ram the gates of the harbour, release the commandos on board to destroy vital installations on shore and later explode, with luck destroying the dock caisson. To accompany *Campbeltown* were two destroyers, a motor gun boat, sixteen motor launches and a motor torpedo boat *MTB 74*, commanded by Micky Wynn, which carried two delayed-action torpedoes to be fired at the dock caisson in the event of *Campbeltown*'s failing in her task. On 28 March 1942 the Chariot flotilla sailed from Falmouth with *MTB 74* towed by *Campbeltown*. They crossed 400 miles of open sea and were three miles up the estuary of the Loire before the Germans opened fire. *Campbeltown*, which was flying the German ensign, immediately replied in German with friendly messages by Morse Code and Aldis lamp. The enemy batteries held their fire, allowing *Campbeltown* to creep closer to its target.

At 1.27 am and closing on the target, *Campbeltown* lowered the German flag and hauled up the British ensign. Under intense fire *Campbeltown* cut through the torpedo net and rammed the dock gates at 1.34 am. Wynn, who had been cast off from *Campbeltown*, now fired his two torpedoes at his secondary target, the gate at the old entrance. Having picked up survivors from *Campbeltown* and another vessel, Wynn was proceeding down the river at full speed (40 knots). Three-quarters of the way down he saw two men on a Carley float directly ahead of him. He had to make a snap decision, either to stop – which could be done quickly – or to drive on, which would have meant that the men would be washed off their float and probably drowned. He was to record later, 'it was an awful decision …I decided to stop the vessel and we pulled up right alongside them. My crew had got hold of them, but unfortunately at that very moment the German shore batteries found their mark and two shells went straight through us.' Wynn was blown from the bridge down to the bilges. Only the presence of mind of his chief motor mechanic, Chief Petty Officer Lovegrove, who decided to search that area before jumping overboard, saved him. He held the severely injured Wynn, with one eye hanging from its socket and peppered with shrapnel, as they made their way to the other survivors on a Carley float. In the intense cold the men began to slip away: when the Germans found them 12 hours later there were only three left out of thirty-six.

That morning, after hours of chaos, a number of German officers and technicians were inspecting *Campbeltown* just as her five tonnes of ammonal blew up, rendering the dock completely useless. Two days later, just when the Germans thought it was all over, Wynn's two well-placed torpedoes exploded and blew the gates of the old entrance to pieces. Now a prisoner of war and blinded in one eye, Wynn had the satisfaction of hearing the explosion. Five Victoria Crosses were awarded for this daring raid. Wynn was awarded the Distinguished Service Cross.

Wynn found himself as a prisoner of war at Marlag Nord POW camp. His captors, without the use of anaesthetic, amputated his mangled finger and removed his damaged eye from its socket. Kindly enough, they gave him a German-made glass replacement. After several escape attempts and causing sufficient trouble to earn the nickname 'Wicked Wynn', he was transferred to the notorious and more secure Colditz POW camp in 1943. Wynn looked a frightening sight: a steel finger, eye patch and wounds across his body from the shrapnel, but he wasn't in any pain. Nevertheless, Wynn realized that his physical appearance was his ticket to escape, so he hammed it up beautifully. Finding some crutches from the old hospital at Colditz he often screamed in pain whilst hobbling around the Castle to give the Germans a reminder of his ill-health. Wisely, he was 'too unwell' to embark on any escape attempts but helped with escapes whenever he could across the different nationalities in Colditz. Wynn was sent to a hospital in Leipzig for tests, where he found a cellar where he could throw off the crutches and run up and down to keep fit. Sadly for Wynn the German medics did not find anything wrong with him and he was returned to Colditz and to 'work his ticket' as it was known. The following year news reached Colditz of a visit from the Medical Commission to view sick or injured prisoners of war for repatriation to the United Kingdom. With a false eye, a steel finger and some credible acting Wynn got himself onto the list and was passed for repatriation home which eventually came in January 1945.

On arrival back in England he immediately volunteered again for active service, only to be told that if he returned to Germany he would be shot as a prisoner who had escaped. Wynn decided to ignore this advice and whilst in Germany heard that Lovegrove, the man who had saved his life at St Nazaire, was held in a German naval camp. Wynn volunteered to join the relieving force and was delighted to be reunited with the man who saved his life at St Nazaire. Every prisoner of war after hostilities ended wanted to find a guard who had been unkind, in Wynn's case it was Chief Security Officer Gussveld who had made his life difficult. Gussveld had been located in his officer's uniform and captured by American troops, Wynn and a number of other prisoners that had been newly liberated gave him a taste of his own medicine. With the score settled, they left Gussveld to the American GIs.

After the war Wynn returned to farming, and in 1963 became High Sheriff of Merionethshire. Two years later he succeeded his father as Lord Newborough and inherited 20,000 acres in North Wales. In 1971, to meet the increasing cost of taxation he was forced to sell Bardsey Island, which had been owned by his family since the time of Henry VIII. Wynn would still return to Germany in his later years, mainly to have a new glass eye fitted as he could not find one of similar quality in Britain. Robert Charles Michael Wynn, Naval Officer and farmer: born 24 April 1917; DSC 1942; succeeded in 1965 as seventh Baron Newborough and High Sheriff of Merionethshire (1963) died in Istanbul on 11 October 1998. After repatriation his ashes were fired from an eighteenth-century cannon on his estate at Rhug.

Major Pat Reid – United Kingdom

The name Major Pat Reid is synonymous with the Colditz Castle legend after two books penned by Reid and a successful 1970s board game 'Escape from Colditz', all of which gave birth to the classic BBC series *Colditz* starring Robert Wagner. Reid was born in India in November 1910 to Irish parents and was educated at St Dominic's Preparatory School in Dublin and later

King's College London, training as a civil engineer. It was in 1933 that he joined the Territorial Army as a Second Lieutenant and when the Second World War broke out he was mobilized for active service with the British Expeditionary Force during the Battle for France. The swift advance of German forces near Cassel surrounded British troops and Reid was captured and sent to Laufen Castle in Bavaria. Within weeks he and other officers had dug a tunnel over 22ft in length and promptly absconded. The plan was to reach Yugoslavia, just 150 miles away.

The party included five others, Rupert Barry, Harry Elliot, Peter Allan, Kenneth Lockwood and Dick Howe. They left Laufen at 6:30 am on 5 September 1940 and covered 50 miles on foot until the mountains of Radstadt in Austria forced the men to use roads. Locals saw the group and engaged them, and with no papers and only one of the group fluent in German, it was a hopeless case. Reid was rewarded with a month of solitary confinement and just bread and water to live off. All six were branded 'troublemakers' by German authorities and despatched to the escape-proof Oflag IV-C. Reid arrived at Colditz as one of the first prisoners and the imposing medieval castle certainly left an impression that escaping was going to be a real challenge. He began to survey the building for weaknesses, at first concentrating on areas of the Castle that the British did not use. With the help of a Polish Lieutenant, Miki Surmanovicz, Reid was soon able to open doors without the use of keys, using metal wire and developed considerable skill in lockpicking. Reid saw a weakness in the prisoner of war shop which sold razor blades and other basic items as there was a manhole drain cover behind the counter. Many years ago a new building had been constructed over part of the existing inner courtyard and the drain which was now inside the shop. Working under the supervision of a German Feldwebel, Captain Kenneth Lockwood had already ensconced himself in the room as 'assistant manager' and accountant. This had initially nothing to do with generating any escape opportunities. Lockwood had a background with figures as he had worked on the London Stock Exchange before the outbreak of war and keeping the accounts helped pass the time and occupy him in an area he had an affinity with, this gave Reid the cover he needed for a look down the manhole. A suitable distraction was created for the Feldwebel and the initial inspection revealed that there were tunnels leading in two directions, one connecting with a tunnel he had already noticed in the Castle yard, and another leading out under the floor by the window. A second check revealed that this route was around 18 yards long and built with a curve, a pile of large stones and mortar blocked the way through. Using his skill as a civil engineer Reid established the drain appeared outside the Castle wall on a supporting bank of earth. Below the retaining wall was a 25ft drop, which led down the valley containing the POWs' football area. After that, the last obstacle would be the 12ft wall of the Castle park and the barbed wire on top.

With the help of Surmanovicz and a fellow Polish officer, Chmiel, the men began to prepare the drain for escape. A key was made for the door from a metal bed frame in the British quarters and to minimize noise problems and the chance of discovery the men worked only at night. A detailed system of lookouts was established to ensure the sentries were at the far end of their section before rubble was moved. After a few weeks the party had made a vertical shaft which brought the tunnel up to the grass and reinforced the top with a trap door just below the surface. Reid, Surmanovicz and Chmiel crept out of their quarters at 11 pm and began their escape with some good fortune, as the courtyard searchlights were not working. The two Polish officers had to descend by knotted sheet toward the courtyard from a high window, Surmanovicz wore plimsolls for the descent, whilst Chmiel had a heavier style of boot. These made a noise as they scraped against the wall on the descent. It was loud enough to wake up the duty officer asleep in the guard house. He opened the window and instantly spotted the makeshift rope dangling alongside. A dark figure was hanging only a few yards below. The duty officer drew his pistol and shouted '*Hände hoch*' (hands up). When there was no response, the officer called out the guard, the tunnel was swiftly discovered, and the escape attempt was at an end. However, Reid had learned some valuable lessons.

If escape from Colditz was to be a realistic possibility, the prisoners realized they must organize themselves with German money, identity cards, suitcases, maps and civilian clothes to have a good chance of a 'home run'. An Escape Committee was formed with an Escape Officer from each nationality to co-ordinate plans for a break-out; the prisoners would work together. Reid was appointed the Escape Officer for the British contingent and successfully supported Neave and Luteyn in January 1942 as they left the Castle through the gatehouse dressed as German officers. By September of that year Reid was keen to return to the ranks after the escape season of the summer was complete, as the Escape Officer could nit himself participate in escapes. Dick Howe visited him in late September and mentioned a scheme hatched by Billie Stephens and Ronnie Littledale which involved breaking into the kitchen in the central courtyard and escaping through the exterior courtyard on the far side of the kitchen. The officers would then climb over flat roofs in direct view of the Kommandantur building to a small pit …and that was all they had. Reid replied that the scheme was the work of a lunatic, to which Howe did not disagree but asked if Reid would join the party with Hank Wardle to make sure Stephens and Littledale didn't get into any trouble.

Reid wondered if escape was possible from the far side of the outer courtyard and sought to contact Dominic Bruce who had just been foiled in an escape attempt in that area of the Castle but was doing a month of solitary for his efforts. Reid smuggled a message hidden in his evening meal and Bruce replied that the buildings in that area had iron bars on the windows. If those could be breached it was possible to lower men down into the moat. Reconnaissance was now required on the kitchen windows, Reid broke in with the help of a distraction one evening and examined the bars as well as the route across the flat roofs. The bar was solidly attached to the frame of the window but the roofs were passable if the party were silent and used a signal system for when the sentries' backs were turned. Upon returning to the British quarters Reid visited Wally Hammond who designed a Colditz bar and bolt press which attached to the sill of the window and when turned the bolt gently applied pressure to the bar and forced it from its position. Borrowing this device Reid snuck into the kitchen on five successive evenings to work on the bar, only turning the bolt when the sentry was at the farthest point from his position. On the fifth night the bar came free and Reid reattached it with black clay.

Meanwhile preparations for the escape were in full swing with identity papers and back stories developed. Reid would travel with Wardle and Stephens and Littledale were the second pair. Acting as Flemish workers reassigned near the Swiss border, Reid and Wardle could successfully pass off their poor German and bad French. It was unlikely they would bump into anyone fluent in Flemish, especially German guards at train stations.

Maps would not be taken. Reid asked all of the party to memorize maps from Colditz to the Swiss border. Civilian clothes were made: Reid had a cloth cap, dyed RAF trousers and an overcoat from a bribed guard inside the Castle, he also had a pair of boots. To scale the flat roofs socks would be worn over their boots to avoid the errors of Reid's first escape with Surmanovicz and Chmiel. Douglas Bader volunteered to conduct the orchestra from a window which had a view of the outer courtyard, thus the music would cease when guards or the sentry were facing the escape party.

On 14 October, after evening *Appel* (roll call), the party of four made the dash across the courtyard to the kitchen window with Malcom McColm as a watchman. The party made it into the kitchens and prised the iron bar back at the window overlooking the outer courtyard, Reid and Wardle went first across the flat roofs and dropped to the ground. With the orchestra as the signal to move and stop Reid was progressing well but then Bader stopped the orchestra abruptly. The he heard German voices: it was the duty officer on his rounds questioning the sentry. Reid dared not move. The orchestra began again briefly but Reid was caught napping. Then silence, no music for over an hour with Reid waiting. It was clear after so long something had gone wrong for Bader and his musicians, Reid decided he should find somewhere to hide, being out in the open was too dangerous, Reid saw a door and gently tried the handle and the two men silently stepped in and rested for an hour. Whilst all this was taking place Littledale and Stephens remained at the kitchen window waiting for the moment to move on.

When the hour was up Reid and Wardle crept out and stole a glance around the corner to see a sentry on his beat. Each man had thick woollen socks over their shoes and this muffled the noise as they crept across the path with the sentry's back turned, a lesson learned from Chmiel's failed escape, and the pair settled into a shrubbery near the Kommandantur building. At last, Littledale and Stephens received the signal to move and soon joined them in the bushes. The next job was for Reid and his instruments to pick the lock on the building where Dominic Bruce had attempted escape before his recapture, Reid moved silently to the door and pulled out his lock picks to begin work, but after a few minutes Priem stumbled back into the Castle after a night out on the town. Fortunately, the German was not in the most observant of conditions and Reid managed to return to the cover of bushes just before Priem came around the corner. Once the Castle became silent again Reid returned to the lock but after an hour he gave up and returned to the men with the bad news, the men would have to find another way out. It was now 11.00 pm.

In the darkness the men whispered to each other and decided that the best chance of escape was to find a room in the side of the courtyard from which Dominic Bruce had attempted to escape and find a way to the outer side of the Castle from there. They crawled across the courtyard to the far corner and in the darkness felt stone steps moving downward to a door. They were in luck: the door opened and they entered. It was pitch black with a small chink of light at the far end, Reid noticed it was a flue to the outside which acted as a ventilation shaft. At first the party believed it was too small to squeeze through but Reid, as a civil engineer, was undaunted, Wardle pushed Reid up as far as he could but it was too difficult. Removing his clothes proved to make it easier to squeeze up the flue, he slowly eased his way up to the surface of the ground on the outside of the Castle wall. At the top of the flue Reid was greeted by a grate of old rusty bars which he quickly bent back double and managed to clamber onto a grass terrace which dropped down three times toward the old moat. With the sheet rope tied to his ankle he slowly pulled up his clothes and suitcase as the other men stripped naked ready to take their turn. Reid surveyed the area, the terrace was 2ft wide with a drop of about 12ft down toward the old moat. By 3.00 am all four men were out of the flue, fully dressed and ready to lower each down the terraces toward the ancient dry moat. They followed the path past the married quarters and scaled the perimeter wall, it was 5:15 am when they finally escaped the Castle. Shaking hands and wishing each other well, Reid and Wardle set off to cross the River Hulde and caught a train from Penig to Zwickau. As Wardle and Reid moved further away from the Castle they relaxed into their roles as civilians more, the men reached Munich and enjoyed a coupon-free meal at Munich station; potato and vegetable soup. Despite the difficulties escaping the Castle Reid and Wardle enjoyed an event free rail journey toward the Swiss border, the Flemish identification papers and natural language barrier proved a masterstroke.

When they left Tuttlingen station and began their walk to freedom on 18 October, Reid and Wardle took a road toward the south-east which led them to a heavily camouflaged factory in the early morning. Immediately retreating, the men had a narrow escape as the guards had not seen them. The men moved across country using a brass button compass to navigate. A forester observed them through the woodland whilst he ate his lunch, and Wardle and Reid moved quickly to out un him. As they crossed the open hills between Hilzingen and Singen a cycle patrol stopped them at a small track demanding an explanation as well as their identity papers, and these were satisfactorily given. Once out of sight of the sentry Wardle describes moving west along the country track, along the tree line of woods and they crossed a double-track railway which brought them to the Singen-Gottmadingen road at 6.00 pm. Remaining at the side of the road until a period when traffic was light, they crossed the road quietly and hid in bushes on the other side. At 8.00 pm on 18 October Reid and Wardle walked into the village of Ramsen, Switzerland as free men and gave themselves up in the local police station.

Reinhold Eggers was returning from a conference to discuss the use of prisoners of war in factories across Germany as slave labour. Arriving at the train station in Dobeln and witnessing long queues for identity checks, his heart sank: he knew without asking but the reply came from a guard, 'Yes, four prisoners have escaped from your Sonderlager.' In November Reid sent a postcard to Rupert Barry who often referred to Wardle as Murgatroyd. it read:

> We are having a holiday here (in Switzerland) and are sorry you are not with us. Give our dear love to your friend Dick. Love from
> Harriet and Phyllis Murgatroyd

The heavily emphasised **H** and **P** were codenames for Hank and Pat.

Captain Harry Elliot – United Kingdom

Feelings within the Castle of Colditz began to gradually change over 1944 as the men from both sides of the conflict realized that they might be fortunate enough to live through the Second World War in 25 years.

For the prisoners this meant a less desperate approach to escaping with some naturally prepared to bide their time and work on the next stage of the war, ensuring that the Castle fell into British or American hands and that bloodshed was minimal. Guards were much more convivial as the protection of the Third Reich was dwindling before their eyes and their future would rest on the word of the prisoners before much longer. With contraband manufactured radios gathering intelligence, the men were well informed and after the successful D-Day landings some escape attempts were shelved permanently. Captain Harry Elliot however, was a man who still wanted to escape. A member of the Laufen Six, named after the camp where they made their first escape, Oflag VII-C, he was one of the first British officers incarcerated in Colditz. Alongside Kenneth Lockwood, Pat Reid, Peter Allan, Dick Howe and Rupert Barry, Elliot entered the Castle on 7 November 1940.

As early as the autumn of 1941 Harry had been unwell and requested repatriation on medical grounds for a number of ailments. This was not uncommon in Colditz but it was a delicate position to be in, Harry could not very well embark on an escape attempt as the guards would naturally point out that he was 'fit enough to attempt escape'. Harry had to be patient and 'work his ticket'. Beginning with duodenal ulcers, the symptoms of which he had studied at length, Harry was the epitome of ill-health, writhing with pain and losing weight quickly. The latter was a subtle ruse which involved two hanging bags of sand inside his trouser legs. When weighed he would release enough grains of sand to show progressive and consistent weight loss. The Germans were unmoved. Unperturbed Harry painted the skin around his eyes with a homemade remedy of carbon and yellow ochre leaving his skin permanently marked with a sallow, hangdog appearance. With no sand left to lose and complaining of terrible pain, the Germans sent him to a hospital in Elsterhorst in February 1942. Harry built a rapport with two Indian doctors being forced to work in the German hospital, confiding in them his plan to return back to Britain. They provided him with a 'terrible prognosis' from his blood tests. In the bed next to Harry was a Frenchman named Lieutenant Lejeune and together they hatched a back-up plan to escape from Elsterhorst hospital, acquiring civilian clothes and a strategy to 'exercise' together and slip out of a side door to the open street. The morning before their attempt was planned to go ahead, the whole contingent of Colditz prisoners at the hospital were roused from their beds and taken by heavy guard on a march to the train station, to return to the Castle. To make things worse, Harry's new blood tests were given short shrift by the German medics.

Upon returning to Colditz Harry decided to lay low for a while, being increasingly troubled by a fall whilst trying to escape from a camp prior to his incarceration in Oflag IV-C. X-ray plates showed arthritis had formed and he was becoming physically impaired, but still the guards remained unmoved. Despite already being thinner than a garden rake he lost two more stone (sand) and went on hunger strike for a week, after seven days Harry could barely walk and received warnings about his health if he persisted with this type of escape. Eventually the German medics relented and sent him back to Elsterhorst hospital. By now there were some captured English doctors working at the hospital and Harry confided in a radiologist who managed to produce a set of X-rays which showed some really juicy ulcers and a medical prognosis of misery which got Harry a place before the Mixed Medical Commission. Throughout the war no representative from the Geneva Convention had been permitted to set foot in the Castle but on 6 May 1944 the Kommandant was informed they would arrive led by Dr von Erlach. This was a clear sign that Germany were losing the war. Harry and another prisoner, Lieutenant Silverwood-Cope, who suffered with thrombosis of the leg, realized this was their chance. To ensure they appeared in the worst physical state possible they spent all night walking up and down eighty stone steps which led up to their quarters at 20-minute intervals to a point of exhaustion. Harry appeared before the Commission in the afternoon as a bona fide case who struggled to stand upright, finally after three years of 'working his ticket'. Harry was repatriated home to the United Kingdom and rewarded with a commission as major in 1948.

Major Ronald Littledale – United Kingdom

Top of Form

Ronald Littledale was born in June 1902 at Sandiway House, Hartford, the only son of Captain John Bolton and Clara (nee Stevenson) Littledale. Ronald attended St Aubyn's school in Rottingdean and then Eton College from 1915 to 1919. Littledale attended the Royal Military College at Sandhurst and received a commission into the King's Royal Rifle Corps. He served in the army of occupation on the Rhine, and from 1924 to 1928 he was stationed in India. He also saw service in Palestine and Northern Ireland. In February 1940 he was promoted to Major, and in May 1940 was Transport Officer with the 30th Infantry Brigade during the defence of Calais. During the Battle for France he was captured near the harbour on 26 May 1940.

As the Transport Officer of the 30th Infantry Brigade at Calais, Littledale received a radio message instructing him to collect petrol and to deliver it to tanks outside the city. When he returned to Calais Littledale could find no trace of Brigade HQ and moved to the port at the harbour mouth. Next morning, while trying to make contact with British troops, he was taken prisoner by a German patrol. With other officers taken at Calais he was marched across France for about ten days. From a small station north-west of Luxembourg, the men were carried by train to Trier, on to Mainz where they stayed for three days, and finally to Fort 8, Stalag XXID. Littledale joined Lieutenant Gris Davies-Scourfield and the 'Red Fox', Mike Sinclair, spending many hours together devising a plan to escape. They had noticed that each day two orderlies carried rubbish in a hand barrow from the Fort into a rubbish pit about 50 yards outside the entrance. The barrow they normally used was too small to hold a man, but as there was a lot of spare wood available they had a larger one made. Captain Laurie was the officer in charge of the orderlies thus engaged and provided Littledale with a good deal of assistance. Sinclair spoke German fluently and had made friendly contact with a young Pole who lived in Posen and worked in the camp, who could help the men gain access to underground safe houses in Poland. One by one the men would be hidden by rubbish in the cart and carried out of the fort gate by Captain Laurie's orderlies. Sinclair would be first and once in the rubbish pile he would wait for the 'all clear' sign given from a window and slip away toward the nearest town. Sinclair would then wait until Littledale and Davies-Scourfield successfully escaped and would meet at the rendezvous at 4.00 pm that afternoon.

On the morning of 28 May Sinclair was carried out to the pit without incident. He was wearing an old French army coat which had been altered and dyed black, a pair of black trousers, and a civilian shirt. Eventually enough rubbish was built up to hide Davies-Scourfield and (finally) Littledale who were taken to the pit. Davies-Scourfield was wearing a Dutch overcoat and a pair of trousers, both dyed black, Littledale was wearing an old mackintosh, a pair of flannel trousers, also dyed black, both with civilian caps. The men had collected a small sum of money (about 180 Reichsmarks) and had managed to obtain a compass each. Sinclair, as first out, would proceed to the Polish helper's address and arrange for him to meet them at a tram terminus about three quarters of a mile from Fort 8, at 4.30 am. Littledale was waiting outside the meeting point and became concerned about a strange Polish man approaching him. Running would give himself away and with limited German and no Polish, he steeled himself for a conversation. As the man moved closer, Littledale felt he recognized him until he blurted out 'Oh it's you!' Gris Scourfield-Davies replied 'Who did you think it was?'. With his new clothes and his handlebar moustache recently shaved off Littledale hadn't recognized him! Sinclair appeared and entered the safe house where that evening they had a magnificent tea of white bread, butter, jam and cakes.

For the next ten days the men hid in a very small room, where only one man could stand at any one time. They were furnished with better civilian clothes and identity cards. Eventually they travelled to Lodz, from here they would move toward the Russian border in individual parties. On 20 June 1941 Littledale set out to cross the Line of Demarcation between the Wartegau and the territory of the General Government of Poland. Littledale was accompanied by a young Pole and travelled by tram to the Eastern outskirts of Lodz, spending the night in a safe house. The following morning they used a horse-drawn cart to reach Borowa and walked to Galkow, where they ate breakfast at a farmhouse with German frontier guards in the village. Fearful of remaining in one place Littledale was moved in stages from house to house until he reached the eastern end. In one of the houses Littledale was reunited with Davies-Scourfield.

On 22 June they met Sinclair and all three were gravely disappointed to hear that the Germans had invaded Russia, making escape toward the border now impossible. An alternative plan was borne, to hide out in Warsaw until a pathway to a port could be arranged. With German guards still searching houses, all three men left at 3.00 am on 23 June 1941 along the main road to Warsaw on foot. On 25 June the men arrived in the city exhausted, hot and hungry. Over the next month the men stayed at various safe houses across the city, Littledale was given good-quality forged identity papers describing him as a farmer. Crucially he had his photograph on them. It was at this point that the three men were forced to split up, Davies-Scourfield remained in Warsaw and was recaptured by the Germans in March 1942. Littledale and Sinclair spoke some German so were given priority to escape. During the evening of 26 August Sinclair and Littledale, together with three Poles, caught the night train to Karkow and remained there for the night. On 27 August the pair caught a train to Zakopane near the border with Slovakia and after dark were guided across the frontier. At 9.00 am on 31 August, the men caught a train for Budapest. All the time the Polish handlers working on the escape line through occupied territory concentrated on the physical appearance of the men, keeping shoe polish, shaving equipment and a change of civilian clothes to ensure respectability. Arriving in Budapest in the late afternoon of the same day they enjoyed a hearty meal, and all of September and some weeks of October were spent hiding in the city. In October Littledale and Sinclair walked across the Hungarian-Yugoslavia frontier and boarded a train at a small station, the aim was to cross the Danube to Belgrade by ferry. This ferry was most carefully controlled by German troops but fortunately one of the party could speak Serbian and there were many travellers trying to board the ferry boat which provided a good distraction for the guards. Littledale was waved through with no request for his identity papers, Sinclair and the Poles were required to produce theirs and their luggage was scrutinized by a German officer. The ferry crossing took three quarters of an hour, all members of the party had identification papers inspected on the Belgrade dock but each was waved through. One of the party took the group to a house where they had a meal and went to sleep. On 16 November Sinclair and Littledale, with a Polish woman in the advanced stage of pregnancy and fluent in Serbian (who was trying to find her husband), set out for Sofia. They were taken in a horse-drawn cart across the Yugoslav-Bulgarian frontier, it had been arranged that another cart was to meet them at this village. The owner of the cart was not at home, and the farmer who was guiding them got hold of a friend to find another cart for the next stage of the journey. While following this man along a country road, about midday on 17 November, they met a Bulgarian Customs official who requested to see their passes and baggage. The Polish girl told Sinclair and Littledale that as they only had Yugoslav identification, it would be wiser to obey him. It was at this stage the party was interviewed by Customs Officials at Pirot and events unravelled quickly. Sinclair, who was fluent in German, explained they were German refugees and the officials summoned the German garrison for aid. Quickly changing tack, Sinclair and the woman said they were Poles, but Littledale could only manage a few phrases. Events then turned near farcical as the party was taken to Sofia to be handed to the Bulgaria CID who insisted they write statements in French, which went quite badly and only served to further increase suspicion. Conditions in the prison at Sofia were appalling: no food was given, only water, and vermin crawled over prisoners in the cramped cells. Sinclair and Littledale stuck to the story that they were Poles, but following lengthy interrogation they were to be handed over to the Germans, including the girl. This was very alarming for Littledale and Sinclair as if their true identity were revealed the heavily pregnant woman could well face a firing squad for helping escaped prisoners of war.

Littledale protested most emphatically at the treatment by the Bulgarians and demanded to see the Chief of Police. During this interview Littledale raised his concerns about being handed to the Germans and explained the girl had nothing to do with himself or Sinclair. The Chief of Police immediately asked 'She is not an agent, is she? She has not done anything against the Germans?' Littledale explained that all she had done was use her knowledge of Balkan languages to help Sinclair and himself to reach Bulgaria. On 2 December the Polish girl, Sinclair and Littledale were taken by train with an escort to Belgrade. Here the girl was handed over to a German soldier. Sinclair and Littledale were then taken to the Military Prison in

Vienna where they remained from early December 1941 until 17 January 1942. At the Military Prison treatment was good and there were a number of Austrian military prisoners and Austrian guards who both expressed their dislike of the Germans.

On the morning of 17 January Sinclair and Littledale were escorted by a Feldwebel (an Austrian) and one soldier to the train station for return to Germany. When the soldier was out of the compartment the Feldwebel told Littledale he disliked the German troops intensely and that the train would eventually stop near Dresden. The men were still in civilian clothes and had their shaving kits with them. An escape was still a possibility as the men reconnoitred the toilet window and broke the supports which held the glass in place, before replacing the glass for easy escape later. Between Prague and Roudnice the train began to slow down. Sinclair, on the plea of visiting the lavatory, left the compartment with the Feldwebel, who remained in the corridor. Littledale followed a few moments afterwards, having asked permission of the private soldier to stand in the corridor beside the Feldwebel 'to get some air'. Littledale and Sinclair left through the window of the lavatory, Sinclair went first and if he was successful he should leave the latch of the lavatory door in a certain position. When Littledale got into the corridor he saw that the latch was in this position and walked past the Feldwebel, entered the lavatory, locked the door and got out of the window, feet first. At this moment the train gathered speed and as Littledale's feet dangled as he hung on the near side of the train there was a touch on his leg and he saw Sinclair below on the step of the train. Together they moved through the buffers that lay between two coaches and as the train approached Roudnice station it slackened speed, and Sinclair dropped off. As he did so a door in the carriage opened and the Feldwebel looked out and saw him. Littledale was crouching out of his sight and was not noticed. Almost immediately afterwards the train stopped and the Feldwebel leaped out and chased Sinclair who was dazed after his fall from the train and was immediately arrested. Two black-uniformed railway police came and began the search with the Feldwebel for Littledale flashing their torches near to the buffers where he was hiding, a timely escape of steam from a pipe fortunately obscured him from their view. Gradually the search party moved on. Littledale was left under the train at the station, freezing cold with no greatcoat, no money or map of the area.

Littledale slipped off the buffers and walked southwards in the extreme December cold. Taking stock of his situation he decided that he needed to find help soon. He walked into Roudnice and decided he would chat to civilians in German and any who replied in Czech or in bad German he would then declare he was a British officer and escaped prisoner of war. If, on the other hand, they replied in good German he would approach some other person. The first man to reply, in poor German, said that he would have to report Littledale to the police, but took no further action. Unperturbed, Littledale moved on to a different area and the second man that passed the language test said that he lived some distance away and could not help. Finally Littledale approached a boy of about 17 who took him to his house, and fetched a relative who had lived in America and spoke English. Littledale travelled with this relative and remained in the house for two nights and was given a large coat and new boots. On the third day Littledale was given some money and an address in Krabcice. On 19 January Littledale arrived at the address and was given a second address in Prague, additional money and instructions to avoid travel by train, Littledale walked by the side of the roads but it seemed too dangerous to hitch a lift with an unknown driver. At 7.00 pm Littledale arrived exhausted by tram in the centre of Prague. At the address he was given the contact was away. Littledale returned to the freezing streets tired, lame and very hungry. With little option he sat in a railway station until after midnight on 20 January and left abruptly as German guards moved through the station checking passes. In a park a short distance from the station Littledale flung himself at a man and told him he was a British officer on the run and needed help. Fortunately the man knew of a restaurant that was warm and he could get some food and a hot drink. When Littledale woke the next morning in the restaurant his helper had vanished.

After breakfast with some money he was left, Littledale again visited the address he had been given and the contact was present and agreed to help. The plan was to hide out in various addresses across the city and reach Switzerland over the mountains when the snow had melted in early spring. After successfully hiding until 18 May, it was decided to put the plan into action. A guide took Littledale by train to Husinec and two days later a second helper travelled with Littledale to Linz by train staying in a safe house. The following morning Littledale travelled alone to Innsbruck using slow trains (usually third class) and bought tickets in stages to avoid suspicion. Eventually Littledale arrived in Bludenz without a guide, he walked about the town and found an old man working in a garden and asked him about crossing the mountain pass into Switzerland. The man replied that the snow was impassable and that the frontier was very strongly guarded. The downcast Littledale walked to the Lion Hotel and bought himself a beer.

That night Littledale slept in a barn on the outskirts of the town and the following morning travelled to Schruns close to the border. Unsure of his next move he spoke with a priest near a church in the town and asked if crossing into Switzerland was possible. The priest replied that the snow was still heavy and would be too dangerous (it was also confirmed by another civilian). Realizing he had arrived too soon Littledale decided to retrace his steps and lie low in Husinec and return to Schruns in late June when the snow would have melted. The toll of such a long time on the run with limited food put Littledale in a fever for two days just as he reached his helpers in Husinec. On 27 May he felt better but was told that Reinhard Heydrich had been assassinated and police activities had increased greatly; his position was very grave, as it was for Littledale's guides and handlers. Littledale felt the best option was to return to Prague and hide in the city. While trying to board a train at Husinec on 29 May a Czech gendarme asked Littledale for his pass, his luck had run out. With no pass Littledale explained he had lost it but was promptly arrested and handed over to the German Criminal Police in Budweis.

Fingerprints and a photograph were taken before interrogation, and the following day Littledale was taken to Prague, to the Gestapo HQ and feared he would be mixed up in the hunt for those who had assassinated Heydrich. On 31 May an interrogation began which lasted three days, the interrogator asking about routes, safe houses and guides. During this process Littledale felt some relief that he wasn't being mixed up with the Heydrich matter, the Gestapo, from the line of questioning, obviously realizing he was an escaped prisoner of war. For the next six weeks Littledale remained in solitary confinement with the Gestapo. Conditions were poor, a starvation diet and insufficient water in the hot weather. Littledale was forced to drink water from his lavatory bowl in his cell. Finally, he was taken by train on 17 July under escort to Colditz Castle. As a major in his new surroundings Littledale was quickly included in a potential escape plan with Lieutenant Commander William 'Billy' Stephens and a second pair, Major Pat Reid and Flight Lieutenant Hank Wardle. Colditz Castle contained an inner courtyard and an outer one, beyond the latter were some terraces and flat roof buildings housing boilers. If the party could gain entry to the kitchens on the inner courtyard, it opened out onto the outer part of the Castle. The men could then navigate the terraces and old moat and follow a road which passed the married quarters for guards and over a large stone wall to freedom. This route also involved crossing the route of a sentry. The kitchen was entered at night through a window. The attention of the sentries in the inner courtyard was distracted on the four previous nights, which enabled the rivet head of the transverse bars on this window to be cut. The rivet was found to be hot sweated, and the loosening of the bars was only accomplished by means of a press manufactured within the camp. This instrument was constructed from an iron bar, a square thread screw, and soft iron bed slats. The other tools used were a hacksaw and files. The screw pins applied very heavy pressure, forcing the rivet out of the bar. This work was done silently, and without trace, through a window which normally was kept locked by the Germans and which had to be opened to enable the work to be carried out.

On 14 October during the evening Reid and Wardle proceeded on the flat roof thence dropped to the ground (10ft) and waited two hours in a conveniently found door entrance in shadow, owing to the failure of signalling system by accordion music. Finally, they went ahead and crossed the sentry's beat when his back was turned, thence along the front of the Kommandantur terrace. At one point a German soldier passed within a yard of Reid, who was lying flat on a grass border in the open but was not noticed. At the end of the terrace near the carpenter's store Reid and Wardle found a cellar, in which they rested; in the meantime, Littledale and Stephens followed their route and joined them. The door of the carpenter's store could not be unlocked, but an exit was found through an extremely narrow flue running at ground level from the cellar to the outer side of the courtyard buildings. This flue was barred but one bar was successfully loosened. The process of getting through this flue took an hour, during which time no concealment against a patrol was possible. Three stages of terraces, each about 13ft high (a moat in former times) were then descended by the aid of a sheet ladder. The top terrace was within yards of sleeping Germans and the bottom some ten yards from the dog kennels. Twice during the descent an Alsatian dog was roused and barked furiously, but no action was taken. Each of the four members of the party carried attaché cases, which were muffled with shirts and sheets during the process of exit. Though a great hindrance at the time, their contents of civilian clothes etc. were invaluable later. Arriving at the bottom terrace, the party proceeded along the road between the married quarters and then scaled the gate in the wall topped with barbed wire, using homemade snippers. At this point, as arranged previously the party spilt; Reid and Wardle forming one pair and Stephens and Littledale the other. The escape was so successful the guards were alerted to the problem by a local in the town looking up at the Castle who rang the Castle to say she could see sheets dangling from a window.

Littledale and Stephens set off briskly for Rochiltz and caught the 8.05 am train for Chemnitz where the pair were stopped and their papers examined which passed with flying colours. By 11.00 pm the men arrived in Nuremburg and drank beer before sleeping at the station and caught an early train to Stuttgart, it was here that Littledale and Stephens benefitted from previous failed escapes. As booking a ticket which took them to the frontier from a large city appeared suspicious, they deliberately booked short journey train tickets to appear as though they were civilians making a short trip. The final leg of this ploy landed the men in Tuttlingen, but Littledale and Stephens walked out of the town by the wrong road and did not want to risk doubling back as it would look obvious they were lost POWs on the run. Making a rough shelter beneath a tree with leaves around them, the pair spent the night in some woods. On 17 October the men realized their position with the use of a small scale map and a home-made compass, moving on foot across country to the railway station just south of Immendingen they rested until dark in woods. The following day after crossing the railway further north they found the point where the main Hilzingen-Singen road meets the wood, shown to them as leading to the frontier but it eventually became clear that they were going in the wrong direction. Again, Littledale and Stephens hid in woods and looked at the map and compass for guidance. At 9.00 pm they arrived on a frontier road and were challenged by a frontier sentry who examined their papers and was satisfied the men were lost and searching for Singen railway station. eventually they were able to move away. Weak and tired, Littledale and Stephens remained hidden until the moon went down and then crossed to a wood north of Ramsen, where they arrived in the early hours of 20 October. They remained hidden until dawn and then reported to the Swiss police in Ramsen, they had made it to Switzerland.

For bravery and sheer persistence to escape Ronald received the DSO on his return to Britain in May 1943. Of the three years he spent as a prisoner of war, half were spent on the run in enemy territory. He returned to France after D-Day in 1944 and was commanding the 2nd Battalion King's Royal Rifles when he was killed when the jeep he was riding in drove over a landmine on 1 September 1944: he was 42 years of age.

LITTLEDALE.—Killed in action in North-West Europe in Aug., 1944, Lieut.-Col. Ronald Bolton Littledale, D.S.O., King's Royal Rifle Corps. beloved only son of Mrs. Littledale and the late Capt. J. B. Littledale, Bunbury House, Bunbury, Cheshire, aged 42 years.

Lieutenant J.M. Barnett – United Kingdom

The position of Jewish prisoners of war within Colditz, and wider Germany, was very delicate. These men were not discouraged from attempting escape, but if they were recaptured there was the very real possibility of transportation to one of Poland's many death camps. Information had filtered into the Castle about such camps from over-familiar guards. Those who escaped and were recaptured told others of witnessing Germany while on the run and radio broadcasts taken in from the home-made sets hidden throughout the fortress. Lieutenant Barnett was captured early in the war, November 1940, and courtesy of a failed attempt to gain freedom he arrived at Colditz on 4 August 1941. Barnett soon realized escape from Colditz was going to be very challenging.

The phrase 'working their ticket' was coined to describe the men who aimed to gain their freedom before other repatriated men through ill health by simply 'going around the bend' resulting in secure medical deportation to the United Kingdom. The Medical Commission had not reached Colditz despite the war raging for over four years. It was composed of medical officers, one of the belligerent power (Germany) and two Swiss nationals of the Protecting Power of the other belligerent. In May 1944, the miracle happened and Colonel Tod, the Senior British Officer at the time, was informed of the forthcoming visit of the Commission. After some debate Kommandant Prawitt agreed to a list of twenty-nine prisoners being drawn up for submission to the Commission for repatriation on medical grounds, however the Gestapo had the final word. The names of those permitted by the Gestapo to be examined by the Commission for repatriation were announced at the midday *Appel* on 5 May. Six names out of the twenty-nine were omitted. Kommandant Prawitt was tasked with guiding Colditz through these tricky times as Allied victory drew closer. He was a man who enjoyed life and was a regular at dinner parties, often taking two cigars when offered one. Crucially he was in open opposition to Hitler and the prisoners of Colditz were fortunate to have Prawitt as Kommandant. In these last months, tensions inevitably rose inside the Castle as the prisoners scented victory and the guards position became weakened as months passed. Prawitt was a strict disciplinarian with his men, once admonishing a guard for turning up his collar to keep out the snow whilst on duty at night. As far as he was concerned it was business as usual until the day Colditz was handed over to the Allies. Prawitt respected the Geneva Convention and the Medical Commission, he was also aware that the war could be over in a matter of months. The wrong decision was made over Elliot and the other five men, the end of the war could be very difficult.

Colonel Tod stated categorically that either all twenty-nine would appear or none. It was a moment of brinkmanship which escalated the following day, a special roll-call sounded on Saturday the 6th at 9.15 am and the officers paraded. After the count had been checked by the Security Officer Eggers, Hauptmann Püpcke called once more for the twenty-three to step forward. Nobody moved. The Kommandant, Prawitt asked Eggers to speak in English and addressed Colonel Tod: 'Parade the walking cases in front at once, Herr Oberst. Stretcher cases will be inspected later.' The tall, grey-haired Royal Scots Fusilier, standing alone in front of his men, replied coldly: 'Herr Hauptmann, this action of the German High Command is despicable. It is dishonest, unjust and cowardly. The twenty-nine men must be allowed to go forward for examination. I will no longer hold myself responsible for the actions of my officers. The parade from this moment is yours. Take it!'

Barnett, along with many POWs, held his breath. Colonel Tod marched back to the ranks behind him and stood at attention, at the right of the line. Eggers addressed the British prisoners in English and began to harangue the parade: 'British officers, you will remain on parade until those ordered for examination by …' His further words were lost as, with one accord, the parade broke up in disorder and men stamped around the courtyard, drowning his voice with the shuffling of boots and the clatter of wooden clogs on the cobbles. This was mutiny. Within seconds the Riot Squad entered the courtyard with fixed bayonets and followed by three NCOs with revolvers drawn. The latter ploughed into the ranks to identify the sick men and pull them out of the courtyard. A riot ensued which was heard by the waiting officials of the Medical Commission, two Swiss and one German, and they demanded to see the Senior British Officer for an explanation. Colonel Tod was found amongst the melee and met the Commission at 10.30 am, apologizing for his delay and the role he played in the riot. When he explained the actions of the Gestapo and the six men removed from the list, the Commission was amazed and demanded an explanation. Kommandant Prawitt and the German member of the Commission then telephoned to Berlin explaining the condition of these men, including Elliot and how the repatriation of such sick men would hardly assist the Allied war effort. The deadlock was broken – Berlin gave way. At 11.45 am the Commission began its work with Prawitt's guidance and swiftly passed Barnett who returned home to the United Kingdom safely. He had been in captivity for over four years.

Lieutenant Commander William 'Billie' Stephens – Northern Ireland

'100% luck isn't good enough; you need the Devil's luck as well'.

Born in Belfast, Lieutenant Commander William Stephens was affectionately known as 'Billie' and described as handsome with fair hair and a Nelsonian nose who walked as if permanently on the deck of a ship. Born on 9 March 1911, he was the son of a Belfast shipping agent and timber importer. Educated at Shrewsbury School in Shropshire before joining his father's firm, he joined the Royal Naval Volunteer Reserve in 1930 and at the outbreak of the Second World War joined the Coastal Forces. During the raid on St Nazaire on 27 March 1942, Stephens commanded *Motor Launch 192* with considerable skill and bravery. Intelligence reports had indicated that the new German battleship *Tirpitz* had been completed and if she broke out into the Atlantic and then, like *Bismarck*, headed for France, the only dock that could accommodate her was at St Nazaire at the mouth of the River Loire. Operation Chariot was devised: a daring scheme in which the destroyer *Campbeltown*, laden with five tons of explosives, would crash the gates of the dock and destroy them. Accompanying the destroyer *Campbeltown* was an escort of two destroyers and smaller vessels, including 16 motor launches supported by 346 Royal Navy personnel and 265 Commandos. Under intense fire, *Campbeltown* hit the caisson of the lock gate at 1.30 am. Hoping to draw the fire from *Campbeltown* and to inflict further damage by landing commandos, the motor launches had a tough task. Only four returned. Stephens, in one of the leading motor launches was almost abeam of the harbour wall when his ship was hit amidships by gunfire. Completely immobilized and with the petrol compartment on fire, he had no option but to order his men to abandon ship. They managed to swim ashore and carry their wounded but were soon taken prisoner by a patrol.

Stephens and his crew were taken to a courtyard, searched and then lined up against a wall. The men felt certain of their fate, but fortunately an officer arrived to take control. They were then put into an underground store and, even though they had several severely wounded men, were denied water. The prisoners were then taken to Stalag 133 and confined in appalling conditions.

Stephens was sent to Wilhelmshaven and interrogated before being sent to Marlag, from where he made his first escape by promptly forging a service pass and posed as 'Jean Barder', a French electrician, in order to mingle with the other workers who came to maintain the camp each day. Recaptured, he was viewed as a prisoner of war with a persistent risk of escaping. Even on the train to Colditz Stephens attempted to flee. Feigning illness, he gained enough time to separate from his guard and leapt from the moving train and ran into the woodland nearby. The guards chased him once the train had come to a halt, tackling Stephens to the ground and the Commandant at Colditz awarded a suitable punishment; seven days in isolation.

Five weeks later, Stephens and Major Ronnie Littledale had their plan to escape accepted by the Escape Committee in Colditz. The plan included Pat Reid and a fourth man, Flight Lieutenant Howard Wardle. Silently moving across a courtyard they would enter the kitchens, remove a dummy iron bar from the window (the original having been removed) and crawl onto a flat roof. Avoiding sentries they moved to a cellar positioned under the Kommandantur and exited through a small air shaft which opened out into an old dry moat. Reid insisted that each man carry a small suitcase even though these would hinder the escape from the camp. He felt that the suitcase was the hallmark of respectability; the only men travelling without suitcases were fugitives. Wearing balaclavas, gloves and socks over their shoes and carrying their suitcases muffled with blankets containing sheets. Pat Reid led the way through a kitchen window. Each time a sentry turned his back, Reid signalled for one of the others to crawl through. The next move was through a barred window which gave access to flat roofs which were well illuminated: a sentry was only 15 yards away.

The Battle of Britain pilot Douglas Bader was acting as an observer for the evening, conducting the camp orchestra. The system of signalling was organized so when the sentry turned his back toward the kitchen windows of the courtyard the orchestra stopped playing and each of the men would run to the window. Silently crossing the flat roof and open courtyard, the men were confronted with the air shaft which was very small. Stripping themselves naked, they managed to squeeze through. Somewhat bruised, they dressed in a nearby shrubbery. They then strolled nonchalantly past the sleeping sentry in the barracks. They knotted their sheets and dropped, in three stages of 18ft, into a dry moat. While they were doing this Stephens developed a tickle in his throat, which disturbed the dogs – in desperation, he stuffed his mouth full of grass and dirt. The men then climbed the outer wall, which was only 10ft high. At 4.00 am they shook hands, split into two pairs, and Stephens and Littledale set off together.

They walked to a station at Rochlitz and caught the train to Chemnitz. En route to Nuremberg they changed at Hoff, where they sat in the station drinking beer. Warned to keep away from Stuttgart, they travelled on minor rail lines until they reached Tubingen. After two days of walking, they reached the Swiss border which they crossed under cover of darkness. Their journey from Colditz had taken only five days. Once in Switzerland they were given refuge by a family with a daughter named Chou-Chou who would later become Stephens' wife after the war had ended. In June 1940 Stephens crossed the Swiss border and made his way across France and over the Pyrenees into Spain, where once again he was imprisoned. Using his by now well-honed guile, he offered his wristwatch to a guard for a telephone call to the British Embassy in Madrid. He was smuggled out in the boot of a large American car to Gibraltar and from there by air to the UK where he was awarded the Distinguished Service Cross.

After the war Stephens returned to Northern Ireland to continue with the family business and became chairman of Northern Bank and the Northern Ireland Tourist Board as well as Commissioner of Belfast Harbour and High Sheriff of County Down. He was also involved in the Missions to Seamen. A debonair man, full of charisma, he was always immaculate, fit and alert, and had a certain magic and an excitement to him. Devoted to his Swiss wife Chou-Chou who sheltered him after he crossed the Swiss border, they delighted in entertaining their many friends and in playing endless hours of bridge and the French edition of Scrabble. The couple retired to France in the late 1980s. William Lawson Stephens, naval officer and businessman DSC 1942 and Bar 1943, died at Chateauneuf de Grasse, France on 3 August 1997.

Flight Lieutenant Frank 'Errol' Flynn – United Kingdom

In April 1941 Flight Lieutenant Frank 'Errol' Flynn arrived at the Castle with a Canadian gymnast named Dom Thom after they were caught in the act of trying to start a Heinkel in a Luftwaffe hangar in occupied France with the intention of flying back to Britain. Flynn arrived at the peak of preparations for escape season: the spring and summer months offered a much greater chance of escape and he became heavily involved in the Long Room escape from the British quarters. Captain Pat Reid noticed that the other side of the Long Room quarters wall was shared with the German guards' lavatories. A simple plan was devised whereby a hole would be fashioned to appear above the cistern in a cubicle and British officers dressed as workmen would emerge in pairs and walk out of the German quarters and through the gate as civilian workers at intervals. The lavatories were seldom used as only the guard on duty in the guardhouse would use them. With plenty of cubicles, the toilet in question would be blocked and a sign posted on the door. One night the duty guard was relieving himself and heard scratching sounds coming from behind the wall, Hauptmann Priem was sent for and the plan was exposed. Priem decided to enjoy himself at Flynn and Reid's expense, preferring to allow the British officers to tunnel through the wall as it would keep them occupied. The Kommandant even had a small hole bored through a wall in the toilet so the guards could keep a day and night watch over the room, On Sunday 31 July 1941 the observation guard noticed a small lump of plaster drop from above the cistern and shatter on the floor, Flynn was one of twelve British officers primed to flee Colditz, his partner would be Peter Allan and they planned to travel to Switzerland by train. Gently Flynn eased himself through the hole and down onto the toilet, the room was empty, alongside Allan he left the lavatory and crept around the corner and moved downstairs to hear '*Hande Hoch*' and feel a gun barrel poking into his back. The pair were taken to an office and searched, their clothes were donned by two German guards who quickly left the Castle, observed by the British from a window. This meant the Escape Committee believed the escape was good and sent two more out of the Long Room. This continued until all twelve had been captured. Once the flow of officers had run dry the guards burst into the Long Room quarters and searched it thoroughly locating and confiscating forged passes, disguises and civilian clothes, their best haul to date. With Allan and Flynn at the forefront the twelve men were led back to their quarters by laughing guards to the chorus of a rousing French display of support, as was customary when prisoners attempted escape.

Unknown to Flynn he was about to send the answers to the French prisoners' prayers. Throughout 1941 the French prisoners had been tunnelling underneath the Castle with some success, Bernard Cazaumayou being a principal tunnel-man nicknamed the 'Mole'. The main target was the wine cellar which could be reached from the French quarters by breaking into the clock tower attic, dropping through successive floors with homemade ladders and digging horizontally from the basement. It was believed that the crypt could offer means of escape through a small window. Using the iron mechanism from the clock for tools, earth was removed quickly, working only at night as the noise could alert sentries. Cazaumayou realized that even working at night posed difficulties. An air duct from the cellar reached up to the inner courtyard at a 45-degree angle to the chapel door: a sentry at night would hear every sound or see a flicker of light. The Frenchmen worked in silence as they tunnelled through to reach the air duct and then cellar. They were disappointed that the cellar did not lead to the crypt and a few bottles of Tokay (Hungarian wine) were sampled for their efforts. Unperturbed, the French spotted a real opportunity in front of them. At the far end of the large cellar were five boulders; one was removed and a discussion had about where the 'tunnel' could continue. These boulders were left over from the original medieval fortifications which were rock, rubble and primitive concrete. Buoyed by the Tokay the Frenchmen decided to go for it, each night they crept into the ventilation shaft, removed the slab and dropped into the cellar, removed the boulder and began digging. It was exhausting work and exceptionally difficult, some nights the men only managing to dig 18in forward, and after excavating 12ft they were under the crypt and making progress toward a perimeter wall. Cazaumayou then struck on a huge boulder which weighed in the region of 330lbs, immovable with their basic digging tools fashioned from the clock mechanism. To move this boulder required a great deal of skill as the noise alone would alert guards, and dislodging it from the tunnel without causing harm to the men would be very difficult. Pressure was mounting as the Escape Committee were aiming for a festival which took place in September 1941, a Trade Fair in Leipzig which would be the perfect cover for a mass breakout. A tunnel of the kind they were building could allow many French officers to escape with the perfect cover of many people travelling to Leipzig for the event.

As luck would have it 'Errol' Flynn came to the rescue whilst walking around the courtyard he passed by a German workman who had left a crowbar on the floor behind him. Without thought he instinctively picked it up and slipped it into his trouser leg using the lip to rest on his trouser belt. To the 'Mole' it was a sign from God that help came whilst under the crypt, Flynn's crowbar eased the boulder out of position during an air raid and into a 'well' dug in the tunnel floor to catch it, the whole castle seemed to shake from its foundations. Word was passed to Flynn that should the tunnel bear fruition, he would have a reserved place on the breakout for his donation of the crowbar; Flynn contributed again during Sunday services. Cazaumayou had expected to see the crypt after more tunnelling past the boulder only to find a succession of beams which needed sawing through. The first was a 300-year-old oak beam with a rusty joist. The primitive sawing tools made from stolen kitchen knives were very noisy and amplified by the echoes within the crypt. A swift appeal went out for greater attendance at Sunday services and the hymns were sung with great gusto. The Padre was delighted (although not informed of why his services had become so popular), the Polish section even stamping their feet on the floor during their hymns. Sadly for Flynn, September and the Trade Fair passed by as the crypt was never found by the tunnellers, and they came upon the exterior wall some 12ft thick.

Knives, forks and blunt clock instruments would not burrow through 12ft of stone. A society was established named the Société Anonyme du Tunnel which expanded the original nine members led by Cazaumayou, Godfrin and Barras to thirty. Flynn applied to join as his new tunnel had been discovered by the Germans and he was sentenced to 28 days' solitary confinement, which took his overall total to 170 days. Flynn was in danger of missing his chance to escape through the French tunnel as he was continuously in a cell. A meeting was held and a new plan realized which would see a vertical shaft created to drop underneath the Castle wall, which would also allow the tunnel to be hidden by a false panel topped with grass at ground level when the it popped up on the other side of the exterior wall. All this work, with more men involved removing and disposing of large amounts of rubble and soil, created noise and quite a bit of it. Scraping and scratching noises were being heard during the daytime now, but whenever guards got close the POW warning system swung into action and silence was restored. Attics were now bulging with spoil, so much so that a cave-in occurred and smashed a water pipe which led to a shower of soil and water flooding into the French quarters. At this point Reinhold Eggers became extremely worried as an inspection of the attic indicated that the spoil was a mixture of stone, boulder and latterly mud, which must have meant the French were close to completion and clearly beyond the Castle walls. Close inspection of the Castle showed the Flynn's crowbar was not the only thing missing, vast amounts of electrical cable were missing, screws, 300 planks and countless nails. The French got word to Flynn that the escape would be on 17 January, as they were 12ft from a ravine. Flynn had papers, civilian clothes and enough German money to travel by train to the Swiss border.

Panic was setting in for the German guards, as the entrance to the tunnel remained a mystery. On 15 January Sergeant Major Gephard (known as Mussolini by the prisoners of war) was snooping around the clocktower next to the French quarters when he shone his torch down the shaft which housed the pendulum for the clock and could see nothing. On the floor were pebbles and some grit which indicated soil had been passed through the narrow channel, Gephard dropped the pebbles into the shaft and heard a hollow tap as they fell onto the planks rested over the hole dug by the French, the entrance to the tunnel. Gephard picked up a clock weight and dropped it 30ft down toward the planks causing a huge noise, when he shone his torch again the planks were disturbed and he could see a ladder. The gap in the shaft was so small that none of the guards could slip down, they sent for the electrician's apprentice who was a small boy. The boy was lowered down on a rope and in the darkness he suddenly shouted 'There are prisoners here!': the tunnel had been discovered. Eggers and Gephard was rewarded with additional leave, the guards were buoyant and the French, and Frank Flynn, were desperately disappointed. The latter had pinned his hopes on the tunnel and began acting strangely thereafter. The tunnel was 2ft 4in square, 144ft in length and 88ft downward and was dug over 250 days. Over 12,000 square feet of rubble was removed from the attic at a cost of 12,000 Reichsmarks. The French were 28ft short.

Flynn grew desperate and was thrown into solitary once again for yet another failed attempt. In the long hours of isolation Flynn realized there was another way out, to simply 'go round the bend'. The extremes required to convince the suspicious guards were no barrier for Flynn; his first aim was to be sent to another camp from where escape would be much easier. Inspired by the E.H. Jones novel *The Road to En-Dor*, which many of the POW's had read as schoolboys, Flynn decided extreme action was required to get the right attention and be branded one of Colditz's 'madmen'. Jones' tale of pretending to be mad during the First World War involved a fake suicide attempt which would be foiled just in time to save the man in question, Flynn measured the distance between an overhanging pipe in one of the toilets and realized with the right length of rope he could ease the pressure around his neck by placing his foot on the toilet lid. A Frenchman rushed in and cut him down. Flynn was fine but a large red mark around his neck remained as evidence of his mental illness. The Germans kept a close eye on him afterwards and his official POW record was updated.

After a few weeks of observation the guards sent Flynn to another camp to be assessed but it was a strange experience. He was held in solitary but could see some of the camp through his barred window. It was a peculiar sight, people walked around as if in a trance, looking like wild animals. Guards came to sweep out his cell and he caught a glimpse of the opposite cell and a man clasped in a straitjacket was struggling to eat potatoes off his cell floor. Flynn was deeply alarmed and rapidly improved, but fortunately he returned to Colditz after a few weeks, 'cured' of his affliction, but could not give the Escape Committee any information to aid other officers planning to escape. At this point he began to realize that 'working his ticket' was going to be a long haul and as he had come quite far, Flynn decided he should continue with his mental infirmity. For the next year Flynn displayed strange behaviour, which was becoming a challenge as after many years in captivity and with only so much to say to each other a number of prisoners had begun acting oddly. The German guards were wise to many ruses to develop illnesses or disease, for example a prisoner consumed tin foil or ate cigarettes they could mimic tuberculosis or liver failure, MI9 encouraged the policy of 'working your ticket' by sending pills hidden in draughts of chess boards which could ensure the inmate developed the symptoms of jaundice. The guards and medical team were hardened to such cases and viewed it as an afront to their care of the prisoners that one should develop a condition serious enough to warrant repatriation. Despite the competition Flynn was selected to see a psychiatrist in Leipzig with a second POW named Julius Green; this was a strong indicator that both men were being considered for repatriation. While the guard was distracted Flynn decided to launch a brutal attack on Green as the train moved toward the city. The latter was left with facial injuries and both men had their case strengthened. Flynn's behaviour appeared downright dangerous at times, as the men walked through the bombed out streets of Leipzig he managed to embroil himself in a heated argument with German civilians angry at the carpet bombing of Arthur 'Bomber' Harris which had left the Deutsche Credit-Anstalt, Germany's oldest bank, in a pile of rubble and broken bricks. 'Bloody good bombing' shouted Flynn as civilians accosted him and Green for the damage on their homes and city, Flynn followed it up with 'You bastards asked for it!' Green was aghast, as were their guards who did not wish to fend off their angry countrymen. Still seething after the attack in the train carriage, Green confronted Flynn asking 'Do you want to get us lynched, shut up man.' This was the limit for Green, he was convinced that Flynn was insane: he held no regard for his own safety or those around him.

For years Flynn had been acting strangely and in recent months his behaviour had become so erratic that protecting-power officials had been calling for his repatriation. The most frequent visitor was a Rudolf Denzler who was fastidious in his administration and had earned the respect of Colditz prisoners by his diligence and commitment to fairness within the walls of the prison. Denzler was based at the US Embassy in Berlin and oversaw the treatment of all British and American prisoners of war under Nazi control. He worked to ensure the Geneva Convention was respected but could not persuade the Germans to send Flynn home. The psychiatrist passed both Green and Flynn for the Red Cross Medical Commission which was due to visit in May 1944. The full list of prisoners was submitted, the

Gestapo then struck six names from the twenty-nine. Denzler was furious and demanded an explanation. A dispute arose within the prisoners' courtyard which threatened to turn nasty. Revolvers were drawn by the guards keen to enter the baying mob of inmates and physically withdraw those named on the list. The episode was deeply embarrassing when the Senior British Officer refused to lead the men in protest at the decision to remove six men from the Commission list. The Germans were acutely aware that they had lost the war and, in the years to come war crimes tribunals would be established. The men were reinstated. When Green appeared before the Commission things went smoothly despite a Swiss colonel explaining that Green could go home to England, he replied, 'That's no use, I live in Scotland'. It was a short-lived moment of light relief, in the coming months Green would not be released and gradually it dawned on many of the twenty-nine men that they would not be permitted to return to the United Kingdom. After the war Green discovered that he was not released as the Germans believed he had a role in exposing a German spy in the Castle. Another man on the list, Kit Silverwood-Cope, had been brutally tortured by the Gestapo and Denzler would later discover that the Germans did not want him to return home to show the world the brutality of the Nazi regime toward officers of the Allied powers. Even Douglas Bader, who had lost both legs in an accident in 1931, was refused permission to return, despite gaining approval by the Commission. The Wehrmacht argued that his injuries were sustained before the war so Bader could not claim repatriation under the Geneva Convention. Despite this Bader was always treated with great respect by the Germans, on capture Bader was taken to hospital near Saint-Omer and Colonel Galland and his Luftwaffe fighter pilots invited him to see their Bf 109 fighter. As Bader sat in the cockpit he politely asked if he could take the fighter for a flight around the airfield, to which Galland replied through raucous laughter that, on this occasion, it was not possible. Even post-war Bader was revered, upon arriving slightly late at a luncheon for RAF/Luftwaffe pilots he was astonished to see so many attendees, loudly remarking 'I didn't know we left so many of you bastards still alive'. Bader would have to wait until the Castle was relieved by American forces before returning home to Britain.

Frank 'Errol' Flynn was quickly passed for repatriation and requested to pack his bags. After many years he had 'worked his ticket' to freedom;

I remember being taken down to the doors of the Castle and I was left standing outside. And I thought, this is it. I am going. It was an overwhelming feeling to see farther than the walls. And I could feel water trickling down from my eyes, both eyes, not crying – just water pouring down my face. That a memory I have of freedom, that's what freedom can mean. It sounds a bit sentimental, I know, but there we are.

Lieutenant Colonel Miles Reid – United Kingdom

After Pat Reid's escape to Switzerland in October 1942, the British contingent did not deliver a further 'home run' outside medical repatriation. An event in September 1943 had a significant effect on the men as Mike Sinclair, the 'Red Fox', was shot in the chest whilst attempting escape. It was a large-scale operation which would see up to twenty men escape Colditz, the plan was innovative and daring, the brainchild of Dick Howe. An elderly non-commissioned officer by the name of Rothenberger would patrol around the Castle checking on sentries. He was affectionately known as 'Franz Josef' after the Austria emperor whose stout frame and ruddy complexion were the mirror image of the Austrian royal. The 'Red Fox 'studied the movements and mannerisms of Rothenburger and believed that he could pull off the puffy cheeks, enormous ginger moustache and portly gait. Two 'sentries, John Hyde-Thompson and Lance Pope, would relieve the two guards enabling a first wave of twenty men to descend by rope ladder from a window and flee the Castle through the exercise park.

Within the Castle the production of escape materials went into an industrial scale, 'Scarlett' O'Hara and Major W.F. 'Andy' Anderson manufactured a list of equipment including two rifles, holsters, buttons and medals. The perfect uniforms were produced by Rex Harrison and Teddy Barton who was a dab hand with make-up and produced fourteen moustaches before he was satisfied with his work. The actors rehearsed the language, studied the order of command and put the finishing touches to uniforms and make-up. Mike Sinclair remained calm as he walked around the British quarters in the early evening before *Appel*; the date was 2 September 1943.

Miles Reid was born in 1896, the youngest child of Russell Belfrage Reid, who made his fortune in the tea plantations of Ceylon, and was sent to the Royal Naval College at Dartmouth. For Reid this was a very successful period in his life. Winning the King's Medal in 1912 and the Chief Cadet Captain's Award in 1913, he was made mentor to the younger and very shy Prince Albert (later George VI) and thus began a friendship that lasted until the King's death. Reid struggled with seasickness and prior to the First World War he elected to join the Royal Engineers and served at Gallipoli, the Somme, Loos, Ypres and Passchendaele. At Gallipoli he was wounded, a bullet struck him in the thigh, and he was invalided home. Ironically for a man who saw so much action during the war, he was presented with the white feather of cowardice whilst walking through a London park as part of his rehabilitation. On 9 September 1916, under ferocious shell fire on the Somme, he laid telephone cables for which he won an MC and was mentioned in despatches by Field Marshal Haig on 7 April 1918 'for gallant and distinguished service in the field'. Towards the end of the First World War he was Acting Lieutenant Colonel and was reputedly the youngest of that rank in the British Army. In the peacetime of the 1920s and 1930s Reid worked in industry and travelled widely, often to France and Germany where he became fluent in the language and made numerous friends. With Hitler's invasion of Poland Reid offered his services to his country once more but was deemed too old for service in the Second World War. However, Reid was very well connected, and was included in the British Expeditionary Force as a communications officer or 'Phantom', a group of multilingual officers who acted as liaison between generals of the French and British armies. Reid was given the rank of Captain, later Major, and acted as a go-between for Lord Gort and the First French Army. As the Nazi Blitzkrieg encircled the men at Dunkirk, Reid managed to find space on a boat and returned to England. Unperturbed, he was dispatched to Greece and began work in a similar liaison job between the Allied powers. It was here, when commanding men to guard and protect the Corinth Canal, that Reid was captured when their ammunition ran out. Initially he was sent to Tittmoning camp and later Warburg from where he escaped with a Michael Smiley by hiding in bundles of laundry, but they were both recaptured the same day. During interrogation by the Gestapo Reid was accused of spying on Germany for MI5 on his frequent visits throughout the inter-war period, Reid was worried he might be shot. After a short stay at Spanenburg prison Reid had become belligerent during one search by his German guards as he point-blank refused to take his trousers off. Branded a '*Deutschfeindlich*' (hostile toward the Third Reich) and keen escaper, he was sent to Colditz Castle.

Reid arrived a few days after the Franz Josef escape and heard all about the events of 2 September 1943. *Appel* passed normally that evening and the two 'sentries', John Hyde-Thompson and Lance Pope, moved toward the sick bay with Mike Sinclair. An array of stooges were in position throughout the courtyard and Mike Harvey reported that the real Franz Josef had retired to the guardhouse The escape was on. After the initial twenty men in the first wave there were fifteen more prepared in the British quarters ready to move, the Castle was deathly quiet. 'Franz Josef II', Hyde-Thompson and Pope moved out of an upper window dressed in full disguise and lowered themselves by rope to the Castle floor, they moved off and Mike Harvey spoke in hushed tones as he reported 'They have passed the first sentry!'. They moved around the corner and approached the gate, the men crouched below the windows above heard Mike Sinclair give the command to the guards at the gate:

'*Sie sind abgelost, Sie werden Ihre Wache diesem Posten ubergeben. Gehen Sie sofort in die Wachstube! Dort sind Sie notig, denn einige Gefangene sind geflohen.*'

'You are relieved. You will hand over your duties at this post. Go to the guardroom at once. You are needed there, some prisoners have escaped.'

The first sentry did as he was told, and Pope took his place. The second sentry began to move and Franz Jospeh II mounted the cat walk but the second sentry stopped, he explained his orders were to remain at his post. Sinclair demanded the keys to the gate; the sentry complied but still remained at his post, Hyde-Thompson standing beside him. Sinclair repeated his orders, the sentry remained unmoved. It is testimony to Sinclair's selflessness, he, alongside Hyde-Thompson, could have passed through the gate and launched their own escape, but he held firm for the sake of the main party of twenty men ready to pass through the gate. A shouting match was now taking place. Franz Josef II had been asked to show his pass by a sentry, so naturally Sinclair had to act the outraged officer and lived up to the part, four minutes passed whilst the men argued in German, attracting unwanted attention. Dick Howe was cursing, desperately wanting to shout to Sinclair to make a run for it but hoping in vain he could get the sentry moved. Franz Josef's pass was correct but the wrong colour. The sentry stood his ground but was suspicious of Sinclair's German and pressed his alarm. First on the scene was 'Big Bum' to the prisoners but Corporal Pilz to the Germans. The sentry explained his suspicions, Franz Josef was asked for the password and could not answer, Pilz drew his revolver but felt Franz Josef was about to do the same in the dimmed light and without thinking Pilz fired. Sinclair slumped to the ground with a 9mm bullet passing through his chest below the shoulder blade. Rothenburger arrived to place Pope and Hyde-Thompson under arrest, Sinclair remained wounded on the ground and a snap *Appel* was summoned. Anger and hatred poured down the staircases of the British quarters, swiftly word was passed to the Polish and French about the shooting and the *Appel* descended into chaos with shouts of 'murderers' to be heard over roll call. The court of inquiry in Leipzig accepted that Pilz fired his weapon in self-defence, the British held their own inquiry inside Colditz and ruled that Pilz had opened fire when Sinclair had his hands raised. Sinclair made a full recovery, while Pilz was sent to the Eastern Front.

Reid subsequently entered the Castle with a cloud hanging over the British troops. The Franz Josef incident combined with recent news of the successful Allied landings in Italy across the straits of Messina on 4 September 1943 gave a clear indication that German defeat was a matter of time. Escape became less of a burning desire and thoughts turned to the successful handover of the Castle and its prisoners of war. The only successful escape in the remainder of the war which was not a repatriation was Lieutenant William Anderson Millar who is believed to have reached a safe house in Czechoslovakia but was then betrayed and shot by the Gestapo. With Germany losing the war, punishments for escaping increased to include death. In any case approaching his 50th birthday, it was unlikely Reid would be given the support to escape within Colditz, with so many younger and fitter men to choose from, many of which were fluent in German or French the oldest prisoner in the Castle still had an important role to play. Reid helped calm emotions between prisoners and guards after the Franz Josef incident, offering a perspective that was not always achievable within the walls of the Castle, which brought considerable strain for men who had been contained for three years. After just a few days in the Castle he considered that the guards were being teased beyond reasonable measure and sooner or later the Wehrmacht would be strengthened or replaced by SS troops, a scenario which would end in bloodshed. The Senior British Officer Willie Tod, who arrived in May 1944, took a hardline approach, publicly berating a young officer who was disrespectful to a German guard. Orders were swiftly despatched which included better behaviour at all *Appels*. As 1944 rolled through the months, the intelligence gathered through home-made radios informed the prisoners of the success of the D-Day landings, and escapes were actively called off. Guiding the men through the next phase of the war was a delicate operation. Escaping of a different sort took over, men who had begun 'working their ticket' as early as 1941 were still devoting many hours to their cause. The manufacture of the 'Colditz Cock' glider was in full swing, although more as a way of meeting the liberating powers than a legitimate escape. Reid saw an opportunity to add himself to the repatriation list on medical grounds, as he was strictly speaking too old for military service. The Germans accepted the point but politely explained that there was little wrong with him. After some research Reid plumped for angina as it was very difficult to disprove, particularly in war-torn Germany. Only an electrocardiogram machine, which were in their infancy in the 1940s and not available commercially, let alone at a prisoner of war camp, could disprove the condition. To act the part Reid took up a particularly unhealthy diet of black coffee and plenty of cigarettes and began systematic wheezing when climbing stairs. It remains that this alone would have been insufficient for an escape in the middle of the war, however, with Reid's age, and the realization that Germany would lose the war, the perspectives of the Kommandant altered. In addition, the Medical Commission and Denzler were aware that the prisoners would be the victors in the post-war world, ensuring favourable treatment for these men was important for the years to come. Reid was eventually repatriated on health grounds, finally arriving back in England early in 1945. He was appointed MBE in 1949 for his service in Greece and in 1956 he was appointed Deputy Lieutenant of the County of Sussex. Reid passed away on 6 October 1984 at the age of 90, remarkably free of angina.

International Escapes

Lieutenant Airey Neave and Lieutenant Anthony Luteyn –
United Kingdom/Netherlands

Airey Middleton Neave was born at 24 De Vere Gardens, Knightsbridge on 23 January 1916, near Kensington Palace. Neave's father, Sheffield Airey Neave, continued the family tradition of burdening the newborn with surnames, adding to his own with Middleton, the maiden name of his mother Dorothy. From a prominent family, Neave attended Eton, read jurisprudence at Merton College Oxford and served in the Territorial Army as a Second Lieutenant in the Oxfordshire and Buckinghamshire Light Infantry. Whilst studying at Eton in late 1933 he composed a prize-winning essay on the future of European politics which predicted that the Fascist leader of Italy (Mussolini) and the Nazification of Germany by Adolf Hitler's Nazi Party would push Europe to the brink of a second major war in 20 years. When the Second World War broke out in September 1939 Neave was mobilized and sent to France as part of the British Expeditionary Force. Despite his best efforts and those of his men, the Nazi Blitzkrieg swept them up and Neave was taken prisoner.

Captured on 26 May 1940, Neave made an immediate escape attempt and was summarily despatched to Colditz. Neave's first impressions of the Castle, as he walked past walls which rose into the sky and loomed over him, were mixed, Colditz gave the impression of an impregnable fortress to the committed escaper but on arrival he was invited to dinner by an officer dressed in an orange polo-neck jumper with khaki shorts and wooden clogs on his feet. As the Lieutenant sat down to stew and black bread he felt the growing sense he was the latest student in a public school for waifs and strays.

It was only August 1940 when Neave attempted his first escape. The French quarters were being repainted by three civilian painters with one guard stationed to stop the inevitable flow of contraband. Eggers had installed extra security and brass discs with numbers were to be handed in upon leaving, after collection from the gatehouse earlier in the day. After a few weeks of work disc number 26 was missing. Neave, dressed in a dyed green tunic with a forage hat made from a blanket, each beautifully tailored if not precise in colour, moved toward the gatehouse after evening *Appel*. Neave boldly stated in German that he had a message for the Kommandant from Hauptmann Priem and handed over a brass disc – which guards used when leaving the Castle to go into town. The sentry was fooled and Neave shuffled down the alley toward the bicycles. Once the guard looked down at the disc, number 26, he shouted after Neave. Suddenly a group of guards surrounded him and frogmarched him to the Kommandant, who was so impressed with the uniform that he had Neave pose for a photo which he promptly pinned up in the guardroom. The following morning the Kommandant announced at *Appel* that Neave had been sent to 'the Russian Front', to much amusement in the exercise yard. The waiting list for solitary confinement was so long that Neave was transferred to the town police cells. Upon walking out of the gatehouse he noticed a small wicket gate which led up a flight of stairs to a dry moat; Neave knew that beyond the moat was woodland and freedom.

Despite planning his own escapes Neave contributed to other schemes, Captain Pat Reid had organized a canteen tunnel plan which had collected 700 Reichsmarks (about £50 which at the time was quite a sum) to bribe a guard to look the other way whilst he and a number of men passed through the tunnel and out onto the top of the dry moat. The guard was a frequent trader with prisoners, who preferred the Allied cigarettes and used the Red Cross chocolate he gained from exchanges to gain favour with girlfriends in the town. Months of preparation had led to civilian clothes, identity papers, German money and maps. Those with a better grasp of German were given approval to join the party of ten British officers led by Colonel Guy German and two Polish soldiers, Neave had agreed to act as the lookout and diligently found the ideal spot from which to watch the outer castle. High above the sentry and looking across the dry moat was a window which gave enough cover so the guard would not be able to catch a glimpse of him. Reid agreed to pay half the fee to the sentry before the escape and Neave would drop the remaining half from his window after all twelve men had escaped. On

29 May 1941 everything was set, at exactly 9.30 pm that evening the guard would wander down the terrace toward the far end to give Reid and his party ten minutes to escape out of the tunnel manhole and descend the terraces to the pathway at the bottom.

Neave was in position and observing the guard who he suspected of acting in a relaxed way, not in keeping with the tension felt in the British quarters. Unknown to Reid and the British, however, the guard had promptly informed his commanding officer of the bribe. The NCO and ten men were stationed in the guardroom outside the gatehouse, Eggers and his men were stationed in a small room in the Kommandantur building as the door opened out onto the terrace. Neave could not see this door and the tension amongst the German guards was such that an order came that no-one was to open fire unless expressly ordered to do so by an officer. With the guard moving to the far end of the terrace like clockwork, Eggers strained his eyes in the gentle dusk light, all of a sudden a patch of grass moved and grew wooden legs which were followed by a man in civilian clothing. It was Captain Pat Reid! Eggers was on him in a flash, the guard party in the Gatehouse stormed into the canteen to arrest any men dashing back after Reid shouted a warning. Neave was helpless. Eggers had caught twelve officers in total including the Senior British Officer red-handed along with 85 German Reichsmarks, 150lbs of provisions from Red Cross parcels and the very convincing identity papers of all concerned. Eggers was promoted to Captain, and the guard was permitted to keep his bribe, awarded the War Service Cross and granted extra leave. After witnessing events unfold, Neave resolved that he would pursue escape with one other prisoner, someone who spoke fluent German. The prisoners had become aware that Eggers was a threat. Intelligent and resourceful he had created a Museum of Escape with all the contraband confiscated from escapes acting as exhibits to train his guards and others from different camps.

Whilst working on his preparations to escape Lieutenant Neave displayed exemplary standards in Colditz and despite his youthful age, one incident illustrated the spirit of Britishness in confined conditions. At the beginning of 1941, 200 new inmates arrived to heighten tensions in an already-crowded camp, included in this number were 60 officers of Jewish extraction. Some French officers took exception to the new guests and requested Kommandant

Schmidt organize segregated quarters. The anti-Semitism of the 1930s was widespread across Europe and it had seeped into Colditz. Lieutenant Colonel Guy German, the Senior British Officer at the time, believed it was a French affair. Many officers flouted this order and made contact with the Jewish officers, which included Elie de Rothschild and Robert Blum, the son of a former French Prime Minister. Writing after the war Neave recounted his view of events; 'It was difficult to understand why they should respond to racial discrimination, and I never quite fathomed the psychology of the incident. Few of them [the Jews] were keen escape artists, however the behaviour of their fellow officers in a fascist prison camp seemed to me to be outrageous.'

An escape from Colditz involved months of planning and many contacts. Neave devised the scheme to develop a full-dress uniform of a corporal, to be used at twilight, and march out of the Castle gatehouse. Many days were spent perfecting a dye to match the grey of the German uniform and a Polish tailor managed to convert RAF trousers and a tunic to resemble the enemy outfit. Neave managed to bribe a guard to gain an old pair of jackboots and he used foil from Red Cross parcels to manufacture a buckle and 'leather' belt. Neave then had a vital piece of luck. during horseplay in the British quarters one of the gramophone records slipped off a table and shattered. Amongst the broken pieces the men noticed a small fragment of paper inside the record, when retrieved it was unfolded to reveal a map – a map of the Swiss frontier. The men then set about smashing all the records but sadly were disappointed that no other maps were hidden inside, one officer noticed a small square on the record containing the map which was absent on the others. Despite the lack of music in the evenings Neave's plan was progressing well. A Dutch forger produced an identity card which was a reasonable imitation. Finally Neave adapted an old ski cap found in the Castle which made a makeshift German cap and he acquired an 'arse-creeper' from Kenneth Lockwood to conceal money. Airey Neave was ready.

Major Pat Reid had spotted that the theatre used by the prisoners was close to the German quarters and the gatehouse. A little exploration under the stage revealed a long chamber room into which Reid lowered himself and walked slowly past old newspapers and crumbled plaster to a door, the door was locked but Reid deduced it opened into the upper floors of the

German gatehouse. It was decided between Reid and the Dutch Escape Officer to combine forces, Neave was selected to escape with Lieutenant Tony Luteyn, who spoke perfect German. Each man had to manufacture a German uniform, Neave acquired a Netherlands Home Army uniform overcoat. Epaulettes were fashioned from linoleum cut from the bathroom floor and painted silver to match the officer's braid. Realizing an officer would be less likely to face a challenge from sentries, Neave promoted himself to Oberleutnant Schwarz and asked 'Scarlett' O'Hara to carve wooden gold stars to denote his rank.

However, buttons were a real issue. Lead was in very short supply and the only source of lead piping was the three toilets which served over forty officers. Pat Reid met with O'Hara and Neave who expressed their distress but understood when Reid explained that he would have a full-scale riot on his hands if he sabotaged one of the toilets. As they spoke O'Hara eyed the alcohol still which was bubbling away in the corner producing alcohol for the Christmas party. Reid took fright, 'What are you looking at? I hope you're not hinting!' After a discussion of options it was decided to dismantle the still and the lead coil was melted down and poured into white clay moulds carved by a Dutch officer. The belt and leggings were made of cardboard and the finishing touch of an officer's cap was converted from Neave's own uniform cap by Squadron Leader Brian Paddon. Escape in winter offered additional challenges, the cold weather making survival at night a real challenge and trains at Christmas increasing to aid German troops to reach home for the festivities. Neave was anxious to make his bid for freedom, Reid told him to keep his hair on, the escape was planned in early January. On being dismissed Neave and Luteyn mingled with senior officers and went to the theatre. The men broke through the stage floor and unlocked the door at the end of the passage before stepping into the gatehouse attic. The officers discarded their British uniforms and Reid fought with the obstinate lock, at one point he admitted that he could not open it, eventually the heavy door creaked open. Reid told Luteyn and Neave they must not move for exactly eleven minutes, the time Reid required to return to the British quarters. Neave agreed but added that they would not hang around. Once through the door Reid reminded them of their 'escape theatre'. In view of the guards at the bottom of the gatehouse they would calmly step out into the night air, exchange remarks and slowly put on their gloves. As luck would have it, a German soldier in the room below (the German quarters above the gatehouse) turned on a radio which muffled the steps of Neave and Luteyn as they moved slowly down the stairs. In the evening light the German soldiers jumped to attention and opened the door for 'Oberleutnant Schwarz'. With Luteyn chatting away in German, they moved down the staircase and Neave handed over the small brass disk to the sentry who wished them well as they passed into the night air.

The men strode out into the snow-covered night, Neave doing his best to adopt a Prussian military manner. Unfortunately, despite all his practice he still marched with his hands behind his back, every inch a British officer. Luteyn hissed 'March with your hands at your sides you bloody fool!'. At the outer courtyard the sentry stated there was nothing to report, Luteyn thanked him and ordered him to open the door, which he did. They were now outside the main castle, on the moat bridge from which the wicker gate led toward the German married quarters. A German soldier stumbled down toward them, Neave was startled and ready to run for it. Luteyn, with great presence of mind, barked 'Why do you not salute?!' Open-mouthed the soldier sprang to attention and saluted. At the rear of the married quarters the men scaled the last obstacle, a high stone wall covered with ice and snow. It was here that Luteyn recalled they made their first mistake, Neave was helped onto the top and struggled to heave Luteyn up, being the taller heavier man. After falling down into the snow, Luteyn managed to join Neave atop of the wall and both men jumped 12ft to the ground below. In the cover of trees they discarded their German uniforms and took the appearance of Dutch electrical workers and set off for the town of Leisnig, six miles away. The plan was to reach Leisnig, a manufacturing town where they would be less noticeable and board an early-morning train to Leipzig, 35 miles to the West. Then on to Ulm and Nuremberg before following the Singen route and a walk to freedom over the Swiss border. The moon aided their progress as the snowfall eased, Neave was dressed in a blue jacket fashioned from an officer's uniform of the Chasseurs Alpins, a gift from a Jewish reserve officer in recognition of Neave's support to the Jewish contingent in Colditz. His disguise was completed with RAF trousers, Polish boots and a ski cap made from a stiff blanket.

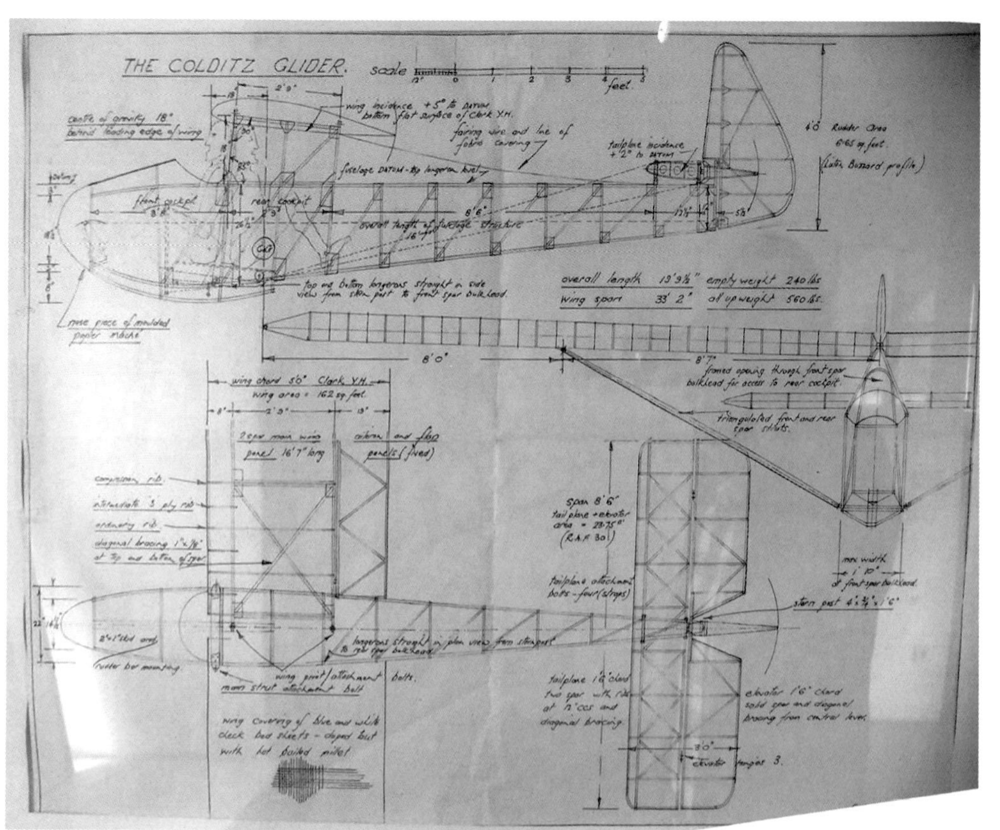

1. The 'Colditz Cock' designed by Bill Goldfinch and Jack Best. (CC BY 2.0/Glen Bowman)

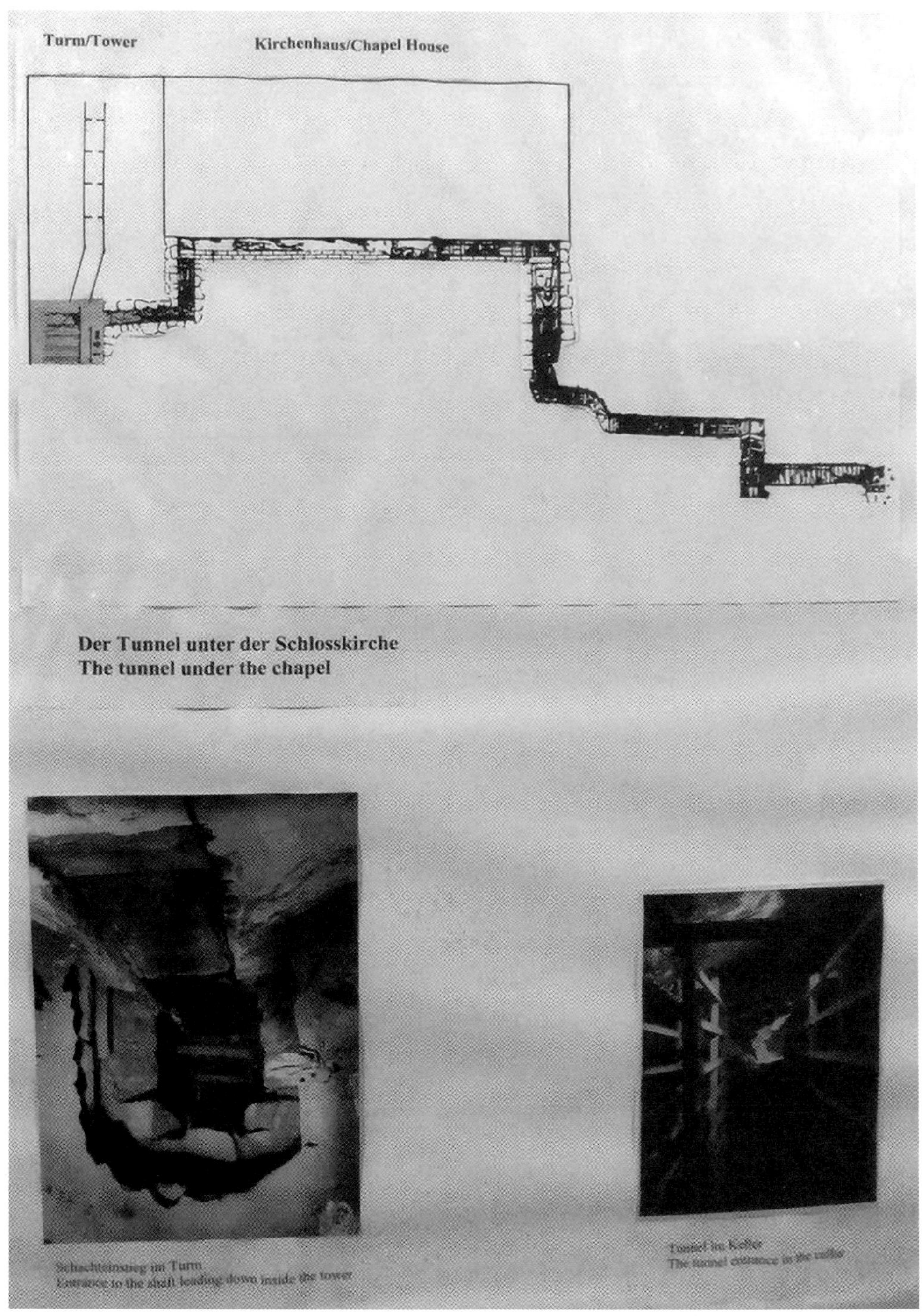

2. A German survey of the French tunnel. (CC BY 2.0/Glen Bowman)

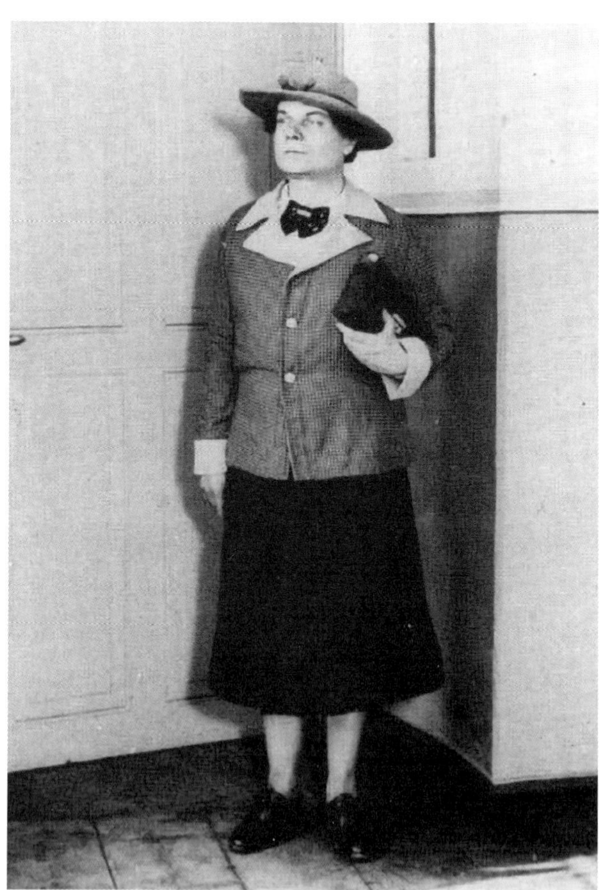

3. Lieutenant Boule's ingenious escape disguise. Boule's wife sent items of clothing individually over many months undetected, enough to make a whole outfit for Boule's escape. The escape was foiled when Squadron Leader Paddon attempted to return 'her' watch which slipped loose. (CC0 1.0/Oflag IV-C security guards)

4. French prisoners pose for a photograph at Colditz. (CC BY-SA 3.0/Alkivar)

5. Christmas at Colditz – note Dr Biren Mazumdar in the middle.

6. The crest of Colditz Castle. (CC BY-SA 2.5/Wikimedia)

7. French scouts held at Colditz. (CC BY-SA 3.0/Philippe Pallu)

8. An aerial photograph of the Castle and grounds. (CC BY 2.0/Glen Bowman)

9. The courtyard at the Castle.

10. The clocktower, from where the extensive French tunnel began. (CC BY-SA 4.0/Johnny Saunderson)

11. Photograph of the dock at the Nuremburg Trials. Hermann Göring boasted that Oflag IV-C was 'escape proof'.

12. The 'Colditz Cock' was to be launched from runners off the attic when a hole was made in the roof and tiles. A bathtub of concrete hurled to the courtyard below would provide propulsion. (CC BY 2.0/ Glen Bowman)

13. Airey Neave's *They Have Their Exits.*
(CC BY 2.0/jhcrawshaw)

14. Douglas Bader in 1955. He supported many escape attempts and ensured morale remained positive in the British contingent. (CC BY 4.0/Ragge Strand)

The men had forged papers and Luteyn had an authentic Dutch passport issued to him in 1936. The two had no papers to transfer to Leisnig but hoped the early hour would ensure a light guard. After two hours of walking they approached Leisnig and saw a sentry so doubled back, entering the town through a different street. Neave recalled it was too cold to talk. They waited until just before the train was due and entered the town, there was no guard at the station and Luteyn exchanged pleasantries in German with other morning travellers. Luteyn bought two workmen's tickets to Leipzig. At 5.45 am the men boarded a train for Leipzig, in the warm fug of the carriage Neave dropped off to sleep and horrified Luteyn when he began murmuring in English before he was sharply kicked in the shins. Once in Leipzig the men decide to wait for the night train toward Ulm at 8.52 pm so they would be able to sleep on the train. They shaved at the station lavatories and bought coffee at the café where Neave made a terrible error of judgment. Unaware of what he was dong he reached into his jacket and pulled out a Red Cross slab of chocolate, the room stopped. The German people had not seen '*tchokolade*' for over two years, much less a Red Cross bar of chocolate. Luteyn shot Neave an angry look as the word '*tchokolade*' rang through the café. Embarrassed, the men left the station and walked the cold streets of Ulm.

Luteyn bought a German newspaper and the pair relaxed in a park, sitting in the winter sun. A girl approached Neave, blonde and attractive, working class with blue eyes. She sat closely to Neave on the bench and said 'Good morning'. Neave did not respond as he dared not get involved in a discussion despite not talking to a woman for nearly two years. Reacting angrily when he did not answer she started to shout at Neave and accused him of being unsociable, Luteyn stepped in and spoke to Neave, '*Hier gehen*' (come here) and the men left the girl cursing in German on the bench. Luteyn recalled 'She was goddam angry'. Seeking a place to hide the men entered a cinema for a few hours. Neave relaxed in the cinema and lit a cigarette, a British POW one, which began to arouse suspicion because of the scent, Luteyn recalled, 'You could see people smelling it in the air, wondering "What the hell is that"? All these things were little mistakes.'

Neave and Luteyn boarded the evening train toward Nuremburg and Ulm on 7 January 1942. The Swiss border was still some distance away and as passengers disembarked space was available in compartments which were warmer. Neave and Luteyn were reluctant, as they did not want to get caught in a chance conversation. To their horror an SS officer beckoned them into his empty compartment and it would have appeared suspicious and rude not to do so. Luteyn put Neave in the corner seat so he could 'sleep' (Neave spoke no German) and Luteyn sat down to speak with the officer, hoping he would avoid detection. Luteyn explained they were Dutch electrical workers travelling toward Ulm, he replied, 'This is how it should be, working for Germany'. The officer informed Luteyn that he was travelling toward Munich and Vienna for a conference as each man relaxed into the conversation. At one point a military policeman walked into the compartment during a search of the train at a station, demanding papers at once. The SS officer waved him out of the door, vouching for Luteyn and Neave's authenticity.

Once at Ulm the men said goodbye and Luteyn and Neave went to buy two tickets for Singen. Despite Luteyn's German passing the challenge of an SS officer the border staff at railway stations were always on high alert and the female booking clerk was suspicious, realizing that Luteyn's German was not authentic. The station police were called, with Luteyn explaining they were Dutch electrical workers travelling on an excursion to see an aunt in Singen. The police officer refused to believe the men and they were marched to the station police office. A senior officer examined their papers, only pausing to be impressed by Luteyn's genuine Dutch passport issued in Batavia (now Jakarta) in the Dutch East Indies in 1936. Neave had no idea how the discussion was going, but the pair were sent under armed guard to a nearby State Labour Office where their story would undoubtedly be exposed. Neave had understood enough of what was happening and on route began eating his *Ausweis* (German identity card) as he realized the Colditz forged document would not stand up to scrutiny in the Labour Office.

Upon arrival the police escort trustingly told Neave and Luteyn to go upstairs to Room 26 and present their papers whilst he arranged quarters. There was no lift so Luteyn led the way upstairs, at the very end of the corridor was an open window, with a metal staircase leading down toward a coal shed. The men ran down the stairs, jumped a fence and disappeared into the streets of Ulm. They crossed the River Donau, unchecked by guards and bought a motoring map before walking toward Singen in freezing temperatures. They walked through a town named Laupheim and bought tram tickets to Stockach, a frontier town as near to the border as they dare travel on public transport. Once aboard they both fell asleep, exhausted from the day, they reached Stockach at 9.00 pm that evening. They then began the walk toward Singen in bitter cold. At one point they met a Frenchman driving a horse and wagon. Neave asked in French if he could turn around and give them a lift to the border. From their bearing he guessed who the men were and replied 'No. It is too dangerous for me, you as officers can have a good time, but if they catch me I will be put somewhere rotten. You can hide. I will not say anything.'

Neave and Luteyn walked all night, and in the early hours they met four German woodcutters making their way through a forest to work. Luteyn told the men they were Poles from a Labour Camp in the vicinity. The woodcutters were not convinced: both men were dishevelled and Neave was struggling against the freezing weather, ready to give himself up. When one woodcutter left on a bike to raise the alarm the remaining men appeared frightened of the desperate POWs in front of them, Neave and Luteyn realized they were scaring the men holding them. Without a second thought Neave and Luteyn sprinted into the woods, and the woodcutters did not follow. After putting some distance between them they collapsed exhausted into the snow. By now Neave was hallucinating. At first he believed he was back at university and then began a conversation with a colonel on the training ground of an army barracks. Luteyn snapped him out of his delirium. With the Swiss border still miles away the men found a woodman's cabin to rest in, they approached by walking backward to give the impression someone had recently left it rather than entered. Climbing through an open window they found a couch, collapsed exhausted under a blanket, and slept until the afternoon. Refreshed but extremely hungry, the men readied themselves for the final push only to find that Luteyn's boots had frozen themselves to the floor of the hut and could not be pulled free. With Neave on one side and Luteyn the other, each man breathed on the boots to slowly melt the ice. Walking west from Singen they saw a signpost for Gottmadingen [4km] and using their small map made for the village of Ramsen in Switzerland. At 1.00 am, the men crawled through deep snow in the fields to pass the frontier, there was no guard or light. It was absolutely quiet apart from their laboured breathing. It was the turn of Luteyn to struggle now, blabbering in Dutch and struggling to move through the snowdrifts, Neave pulled him free and they continued into the night. At 5.00 am the men heard a church bell chime five times and slowly entered a village, Neave saw an advertisement for a circus and by the flame of his cigarette lighter he read that the circus was in Schaffhausen: they were in Ramsen. They had made it.

Neave was ecstatic 'Never in my life, perhaps, will I ever know such a moment of triumph'. Interrogated separately the men explained their escape and were warmly welcomed to the Hotel Schwarn in Schaffhausen where they had a meal of steak and wine. Unused to such pleasantries Neave enjoyed himself so much he got quite drunk and began speaking in meaningless polyglot language, a mix of English, French and German, with some Polish for good measure. The next day Neave wrote two postcards to Colditz, one to the Kommandant Oberst Prawitt which read;

> Dear Oberst,
> I am glad to be able to inform you that my friend and I have arrived safely for our holiday in Switzerland. We had a pleasant journey, suffering the minimum of inconvenience. I hope that you will not get sent to the Russian Front on my account. My regards to Hauptmann Priem.
> Yours sincerely,
> A.M.S. Neave, Lieutenant, Royal Artillery.

The second postcard was written in code to a fellow prisoner in Colditz informing them of the successful escape, although each postcard was not sent for another two weeks, to allow the other officers, Lieutenant Donkers and Hyde-Thomson, time to escape via the same route. Whilst in Switzerland awaiting transport home to Britain, Neave was visited by Colonel Henry Antrobus Cartwright who offered him a post in MI9. As the first British officer to escape Colditz Cartwright wanted Neave to follow a route through France to Marseilles, then to Barcelona and Gibraltar where he would board a ship to Gourock in Scotland. As a guinea pig Neave and a fellow British escaper named Hugh Woollatt would follow a 'ratline' route to HMS *Fidelity* in Gibraltar which would ferry downed RAF pilots and SOE agents. The men were smuggled through a series of safe houses and shared meals with civilians who risked everything to hide the men. Neave was left with a lasting impact of bravery for the women who smuggled him through, stating 'nothing could have expressed more powerfully the spirit of resistance to Hitler'. Meeting these women, especially a Mademoiselle Jeanne who was barely 18 but worked to make Neave and Woollatt comfortable, feeding them coffee and eggs, altered Neave's view of women for the remainder of his life.

On 13 May 1942, Neave arrived at Gourock and travelled to Glasgow by train. Whilst sitting in a restaurant awaiting a train to London he saw his sister, Rosamund, who had been holidaying and was returning home on the same train. Once in London Neave travelled to the Great Central Hotel in Marylebone, requisitioned for MI9. Brigadier Norman Crockett, Head of MI9, recruited Neave to organize ratlines, supply the safe houses with money and communications and repatriate Allied escapees to Britain. With the rank of Captain, later Lieutenant Colonel, Neave travelled into Europe and supported the 'ratlines', later he worked on Operation Marathon which assisted with the rescue of 300 Allied airmen who had been shot down.

Anthony Luteyn served in Australia and Suriname, retiring to The Hague, where he passed away aged 85 in 2003. Airey Neave survived the war and served on the International Military Tribunal at the Nuremburg Trials, Neave investigated Alfried Krupp who was tried and convicted for crimes against humanity for the use of slave labour. In 1953 Neave was elected as the Conservative MP for Abingdon, a position he held until 30 March 1979 when he was assassinated by the Irish National Liberation Army as he drove his Vauxhall Cavalier out of the car park at the Houses of Parliament.

Major Damiaen J van Doorninck and Flight Lieutenant Hedley Fowler – Netherlands/Australia

Damiaen J. van Doorninck was perhaps the most academically qualified resident of Colditz. Fluent in German and English, he lectured in higher mathematics, cosmology and geodesy as well as displaying a fine skill at watch repairs. Such was his proficiency in the latter he established a small business within the Castle for timepiece repairs with considerable variance in prices charged for fellow POWs and German guards. The latter would often pay with snippets of information or German money, vital for potential escapes. In addition to these talents van Doorninck became an expert in picking locks (he had plenty of practice time in confinement) and subsequently developed a precision instrument which would measure a lock using a micrometre to feel for the teeth of a cruciform lock, leaving him with the measurement to produce a perfectly fitting key. The value of this instrument was priceless as soon there was not a lock in the Castle that could not be opened. Thrilled with this new development the Escape Committees which had formed for each nation held in captivity had some rather bad news for the Major, he was too valuable inside Colditz and would not be permitted to escape until he had successfully trained an apprentice. Despite his obvious disappointment van Doorninck diligently spent six months training his replacement.

Hedley Fowler was born on 8 June 1916 at the height of the Great War and educated at Rugby School and was the grandson of South Australia's Premier, Sir Henry Ayers. In 1936 Fowler enlisted in the Australian Air Force before his transfer to the RAF in 1937 as a pilot officer, in England Fowler trained at the RAF training school at Netheravon and was subsequently posted to No. 3 Squadron. After impressing his superiors Fowler served as a fighter pilot with 615 Squadron in October 1939 and converted to Hurricanes and travelled to the Continent for the Battle of France.

Born on 29 August 1902 in Vught, Netherlands, van Doorninck was a lieutenant commander in the Royal Netherlands Navy Reserve and had refused to sign a declaration submitted to the entire Dutch Armed Forces to swear an oath to pacifism for the duration of the war. Sent to Colditz after a failed attempt to escape dressed as a civilian worker, he passed the time there by running lectures on advanced mathematics and geodesy where he met the British Escape Officer Major Pat Reid. The two men became friendly, and Reid recruited the Dutchman for an audacious escape attempt he was planning because van Doorninck was fluent in German and during his time at Colditz had grown a magnificent long red beard, which when shaven for the escape would leave him virtually unrecognizable! Major Reid broke into Sergeant Major Gephard's office (known as Mussolini by the prisoners of war) and realized that if they could tunnel through a wall they would enter a store room which opened out onto a paddock, from where there was only one gate barring the way to freedom. The storeroom was used by orderlies to house timber, old clothes, tools, etc and if the men could establish how often it was used and the change of the sentry they could gather four or five men acting as one NCO and a work party. The only research required was to establish the type of key for the storeroom lock so they could exit and the time the sentries were changed over. A stakeout was arranged from a window overlooking the terrace high up in the Castle, for days sentries were seen patrolling up and down (the time of changeover was diligently recorded) until eventually a guard was seen walking toward the store room with a lever type key. Van Doorninck began work immediately. The summer of 1942 was the high point in escape season as the new Kommandant, Colonel Glaesche, had taken up his new position in the August and immediately a change was evident. Accustomed to instant obedience in his former role as a regimental commander on the Eastern Front, he was faced with *Appels* which bordered on a shambles with officers ignoring the command of the guards, smoking and even waterbombing being a regular occurrence. Glaesche lacked the aggression needed to handle the assembled mob in Colditz and he avoided contact with the prisoners and never inspected the quarters of each nationality. The rapport Colonel Schmidt had built with prisoners which respected the principle that officers would do their duty and escape, and guards would prevent them from doing so, evaporated. New measures were brought in, a new alarm system, machine-gun posts and watchtowers. Far from dissuading officers to escape, they embraced the new challenges and a fresh zeal was created amongst the prisoners. Glaesche was prevented from imposing harsher punishments by the Geneva Convention and the punishment cells were not big enough to house all those who fell foul of his expectations on discipline and behaviour. This created another challenge as the men realized that it was a lot easier escaping the overflow jail in the town's solitary confinement cells as opposed to those in Colditz, so Glaesche created even worse discipline amongst the men. The escape from Gephard's own office by Fowler and Van Doorninck only furthered the embarrassment. After six months he was moved on, returning to his old post on the Eastern Front.

The escape party was expanded to six. Lulu Lawson would travel with a Dutchman named Ted Beets, Wardle with Lieutenant Donkers and Van Doorninck with Bill Fowler; four as Polish orderlies and Van Doorninck as a German NCO; Fowler as a Belgian labourer. September 8th was the night of the escape, and the hole was to be made quickly and replastered and painted so as not to arouse suspicion, Reid and Lieutenant Gill completed the preparations. Just after 7.00 am the group would come out from the storeroom, past sentries that had just started their watch, to the gate where Van Doorninck would, in fluent German, request it be opened so the 'orderlies' could work outside the Castle. Two of the 'orderlies' would carry wooden boxes with tools in for appearances' sake. At 1.00 am an alarm was set off and guards went through corridors checking locks. Lieutenant Priem was giving orders as locks were heard opening and closing down the corridor. Upon reaching Gephard's office all inside froze, then the guard explained that the door was of the office of Oberstabsfeldwebel Gephard, 'Never mind, open!' came the reply. A heavy jangling of keys ensued when Priem exclaimed, 'Ah of course, Herr Gephard has many locks on this door. I had forgotten. Do not open. It is safe.' All eight men took a deep breath.

Between 3.00 am and 6.00 am the hole was completed, materials and equipment passed through and as Reid and Gill worked to patch up the wall, the men rested whilst Van Doorninck kept watch. At 6.00 am Reid and Gill returned to their beds exhausted but ready to assist with the next part of the plan, at *Appel* it was essential that the guards did not realize that six prisoners had escaped. Meanwhile van Doorninck and the five men observed the sentry at 7.00 am who remained steadfastly at his post. Fifteen minutes later the sentry had still not been relieved and the men exchanged worried looks, had they got their timings wrong? At 7.20 am the sentry left to be replaced by a new guard. Van Doorninck had made three keys in addition to the one which opened the storehouse, the remaining three would, he hoped fit the large iron gate which would release them from the perimeter wall. At 7.25 am they made their move. The NCO Van Doorninck left with his work party in tow and was smartly saluted by the two sentries they happened across. The first obstacle was a wicket gate, but thanks to Reid's research the key was hanging next to it and then the escape party had one passageway left to negotiate before tasting freedom. When the group reached the gate, the lock was a much larger one than anticipated and none of van Doorninck's homemade keys would fit. In a moment of brilliance and luck van Doorninck immediately turned around and saw a German guard with a large key, in perfect German he asked 'Have you got the key?' The guard replied, 'Yes, didn't you know?' Van Doorninck replied that he had only been in Colditz a few days and the main guard had explained there was a shorter route through this gate. The guard accepted van Doorninck's reasoning and explained that he was on duty in the nearby sick quarters and he would open the gate if called down to it. Seizing his chance van Doorninck said thank you and explained he knew for next time but would the guard mind opening it for him now. The sentry did just that and the party slowly moved down the path toward the town. As the town grew nearer van Doorninck casually glanced over his shoulder, the guard was still watching them appearing unsure of himself, Van Doorninck whispered to the men to maintain their slow walk until they had cleared the corner. A swift change of clothes and von Doorninck became a German architecture student and Bill Fowler a Belgian forced labourer who had met each other by chance and were travelling to the same location. They wished the others good luck and the three parties set off in different directions.

Back at Colditz work had begun to cover the absence of the six prisoners as morning *Appel* discovered ten men were missing and the gatehouse recorded a night without disturbance. The guards believed this was a prank and when they did a thorough search of the Castle they quickly found two officers, one of whom was Flight Lieutenant Pete Tunstall who was locked in an upstairs room overlooking the courtyard. As the guards were making too much progress, Dick Howe asked if Tunstall could create a diversion and a superb medium pace delivery (water bomb) was lobbed out of the window, landing on the table of identification cards the Germans had just laid out for a formal identity parade. This time the prisoners had really done it. A fully-equipped riot squad broke into the room to drag Tunstall out and he was imprisoned in the cells pending court martial at Leipzig. After a lengthy *Appel*, search parties were finally dispatched at 11.00 am. Van Doorninck and the others had enjoyed a four-hour head start.

That afternoon Eggers was informed of a work party leaving the Castle, and guards traced the departure to the storeroom and quickly located wet plaster. A swift inspection of Gephard's office found more wet plaster and the guards pieced together what had happened. Priem was furious and Gephard became a laughing stock for failing to notice an escape from his very own office. Operation Mousetrap, the standard procedure to recapture escaped prisoners, was launched. Each railway station within 25 miles of Colditz was searched and a cordon placed around it. By nightfall the Germans had captured Lulu Lawton and Ted Beets, and Donkers and Wardle the following morning.

Only Van Doorninck and Fowler had evaded capture. The men had a cover story and posed as two travellers who met at a station, realized they were travelling to the same location and kept each other company on the journey. Bill Fowler was a Belgian forced labourer with limited French and Van Doorninck, posing as a German architecture student, helped him board the correct train. Fluent in German and following the Singen route to the Swiss border, Van Doorninck was confident of reaching Switzerland. Before leaving Colditz the Dutch Escape Officer van den Heuvel had asked van Doorninck if he could discover whether a special permit was required near the Swiss border. The only way to find out was to ask a policeman which would arouse suspicion. Whilst sitting in a pub near the border to pass the time before sneaking into Switzerland that night Fowler noticed a motorbike pull up outside. A Gestapo officer entered and began taking the fingerprints of staff members, a routine requirement of German people living near the border with Switzerland. Once satisfied the officer made his way to the table of Fowler and van Doorninck to request their papers. Fowler 'spoke' little French and no German so van Doorninck helped him with his papers, all forgeries of course, which were given a curt nod by the officer. As he moved away Fowler was astonished to see van Doorninck move after the man and walk toward him before engaging him in conversation. Fowler had not been told of van Doorninck's plan. Fowler's papers stated he was permitted to spend his leave at a farm near Hilsingen where some friends of his were working under the forced labour scheme. Van Doorninck explained to the Gestapo officer that he had stumbled across Fowler struggling with German signs at a train station and, as they were travelling to the same place, kept each other company. Explaining that he did not wish to harm the Reich, van Doorninck asked if Fowler's story was true. The Gestapo officer replied that his papers confirmed this and he was free to travel. Van den Heuvel had the information he required and Fowler, who sat supping his beer throughout, had no idea his liberty had been put at such risk!

Of the six prisoners who escaped, four were recaptured, Van Doorninck and Fowler crossed into Switzerland to freedom. Sadly Flight-Lieutenant Hedley Fowler was killed on active service in March 1944. Major Van Doorninck passed away in Wales in 1987 aged 85.

Polish Escapes

Lieutenant Kroner – Poland

The seventh successful escape from Colditz was made by Lieutenant Kroner, the only Polish officer to regain his freedom from the Castle. The German guards were on high alert, especially after the fury of the high command within Colditz when Lieutenant Just and Bednarski feigned illness to escape in April 1941. The summer of that year witnessed a significant increase in escape activity and Kroner had observed Steinmetz and Larive depart four days earlier. Kroner had been researching illnesses and from speaking with medical officers within Colditz he gathered that gall bladder symptoms were the simplest to replicate.

That summer Kroner had terrible gall bladder pains and the symptoms he displayed were as if from a medical textbook. The Germans were unquestionably suspicious and reluctant to permit Kroner to visit a hospital. However, when examined by the German medical officer his transfer was rubber-stamped. Kroner was taken to the hospital at Konigswartha where his condition improved. At the hospital Kroner was able to accumulate his supplies his escape. He acquired civilian clothing and additional food, and gathered his strength.

The military hospital at Konigswartha was lightly guarded and Kroner made light work of the barbed wire fence and set for the Polish border some eight hours away on foot. Kroner had escaped from Colditz.

Dutch Escapes

Lieutenant Etienne Henri 'Hans' Larive – Netherlands

Hans Larive was born in Singapore on 23 September 1915 and enrolled at the Royal Netherlands Naval College in 1934, graduating three years later and being promoted to sub-lieutenant in 1939. Larive's ship, the *Van Galen*, was sunk by Stuka dive bombers and he was fished out of the water by the Germans. After the German invasion of the Low Countries and the capitulation of Holland on 15 May 1940, the Dutch armed forces were regarded as prisoners of war by the German High Command. At the end of the month, on direct orders from Hitler, a list of terms for release of the Dutch military was given. Conscripts were released immediately, but specific conditions applied to the regular forces. Officers were required to sign a declaration stating that whilst the Netherlands remained in a state of war with the German Reich, they would not take part directly or indirectly in the fight against Germany and neither would they take any form of direct or indirect action which would endanger the Reich. Most Dutch officers and other ranks signed the declaration and were subsequently sent home (many later joined the Resistance). Larive refused point blank and was carted off to a prisoner of war camp but swiftly made a brilliant escape attempt from Oflag VI-A in Soest, Germany, and he came within feet of the Swiss border at Singen. After his arrest he was interrogated by an imposing Gestapo officer who greeted Larive with the words 'This is the Gestapo. You had better speak the truth or we will put you up against the wall, is that clear? One or more of you doesn't make any difference to us.' After an hour of questioning Larive felt he had convinced the officer, who he named 'the Bull', that he was not a spy and was in fact an escaped Dutch officer. Luckily this calmed the Bull as he had been a chef in Holland before the war and was able to reminisce with Larive. When the Bull heard his story of escape he remarked that it was all stupid except leaving the station at Singen, which was a masterstroke. Larive asked 'Why?' and the Bull replied 'Surely you knew that was the last station you could leave a train without showing an identity card?' The Bull continued to advise Larive on what he should have done, remarkably explaining that he should have walked to the border. Larive said that he was unsure if he could have slipped past the defence line and border guards. The Bull exploded, 'Defence line?! Defence against whom? Surely not those damned Swiss? What a crazy idea. There are no defences at all: we haven't got a single man to guard the border! You could have walked straight across.' Producing a map from his draw he spread it out across the table and pointed to the small part of Switzerland that jutted into Germany for three hundred yards, 'You fool!' he said, 'Look.' By now the two men were chatting away about the border and the Bull asked Larive whether he remembered a particular house along the road he walked, at this point Larive pushed his luck and asked the Bull if he could explain where he should have crossed into neutral Switzerland. To his astonishment the Bull explained in detail, 'a quarter of a mile past the house there is a sharp bend leading to a wood, a little further on there was a path leading from the main road and in a few hundred yards you would have been in Switzerland'. This information was priceless. When Larive arrived in Colditz the intelligence was passed to the International Escape Committee and eight officers used the route to escape, four Dutch and four British.

On 24 July 1941, sixty-eight Dutch officers arrived at Colditz. They joined the existing complement of 140 Poles, 50 British and about 250 French. The Dutch officers who walked in to Colditz on 24 July were special men. Principled (all had pledged an oath to the Queen of Netherlands), well organized, resilient, impeccably turned out and with a high standard of discipline; they would create major problems for their captors. Multilingual and German-speakers, the Dutch were quiet and rigorously routine. The enemy was simply unable to glean anything from them via observation or conversation.

Under Senior Officer Major Engles and Escape Officer Captain van den Heuvel, they became a formidable unit. All escape plans were submitted to van den Heuvel for authorization, which was also standard practice for the other nationalities and their respective Escape Officers in Colditz. The Dutch decided on priority and order for escape attempts according to their country's situation in the war at that time. Personnel deemed to be of best and immediate use to the Dutch military were considered first. The nation still had a navy which had stayed operational after Holland fell and a small air force was stationed in Britain.

The new arrivals quickly saw potential in the park exercise ground. Van den Heuvel noticed a concrete manhole top at ground level, covered by a square cover with hinges on one side. About 3ft square, it looked to have a few small air holes and was worth investigating. The next move was to surround the cover, so that the sentries view was blocked and the bolt which secured the cover in position could be removed. A group of Dutchmen casually sat themselves in conversation around the manhole. Some of the men often wore long black cloaks which was part of their uniform and ideal for concealing activity from the enemy. Van den Heuvel managed to remove the bolt and raise the cover a fraction. It looked like a shaft below, which was enough to conceal a man, but the depth was unknown. Further investigation was warranted. On the next exercise in the park van den Heuvel surrounded himself with a similar group of men and managed to lower a stone on the end of some string into the shaft. The depth was calculated at about 8 to 10ft, with a water and a conduit at the bottom. An escape attempt was possible. A glass bolt was manufactured and installed. Two men would use the cover of a rugby scrum to drop into the manhole and wait until dark then break the glass bolt and place the original iron bolt and escape. The new bolt was painted black and installed, observations and information from the exercise periods in the park since 13 August indicated that the Dutch secret may still have been intact. Lieutenants Flanti 'Francis' Steinmetz and Etienne Henri 'Hans' Larive were the chosen men and had made their preparations.

The exercise party arrived at the park as usual and waited in line, whilst the headcount was taken and tallied with the given total before the prisoners left the Castle. The men were let in to the 'sheep pen', a wire-fenced enclosure. It is easy to imagine the scene unfold under the constant scrutiny of the guards. Men sitting or standing talking in groups, others walking around the enclosure as a few decided to run/exercise whilst games of handball or football began. To overcome the problem of the headcount the Dutch devised an ingenious ruse.

Lieutenant Gerrit Dames would settle himself down to lean on the wire fence in the shade of a large tree, a book would rest on his legs as his hands clipped the fence behind him. Simultaneously the handball match would reach a crescendo over the manhole and Dames would move through the wire whilst other officers shook the fence with excitement and shouted 'Run, run!!'

Francis Steinmetz and Hans Larive managed to free the bolt on the manhole cover and slip down into the shaft. The 'handball' circle began to widen again and this was the signal for Dames, who turned around and made ready to creep through a small hole he had made in the fence. Obviously he was seen immediately. He put up his hands in surrender and along with the other prisoners shouted out beyond the fence 'Run, run!!' In the commotion, with two men missing and Dames moving through the hole in the fence the Germans would think he was the third man and two had got out. A full escape alert would be triggered if they were not found quickly. A ground search began, but the hole in the fence and excitement of some brilliant acting by Dutch officers was enough to fool the guards.

Such was the detail of the Dutch planning that Larive and Steinmetz had prepared camouflage in the manhole. A dark grey blanket was part of their escape kit which would he held by the men inside the hole so any guard that did look down would not see them. With freezing water in the lower portion of the hole each man removed his shoes, socks, trousers and underwear whilst they waited for darkness. Steinmetz and Larive were having difficulty holding the blanket above their heads for long periods in the pitch black. The pain in their arms was becoming excruciating and despite summer temperatures, the water was numbingly cold. Clothes draped around the men's shoulders were gradually getting wet as the tired men adjusted position.

In the Castle, a *Sonderappell* (special *Appel*) had identified Larive and Steinmetz as missing. A snap search of the Dutch quarters also found items of civilian clothing and a map with instructions of how to travel from Tuttlingen in south-west Germany and get across the Swiss frontier. This was a significant find. The Germans would need every scrap of information. The *Sonderappell* had revealed three more Dutch officers, Lieutenants Kruimink, van der Krap and van Lynden, were also missing.

Around 10.00 pm Larive and Steinmetz decided to make their move. They exited the shaft, climbed over the wire fence surrounding the enclosure and scaled the 12ft park perimeter wall by climbing a nearby tree. Negotiating barbed wire on top of the wall with the aid of the blanket, they landed safely on the other side and were on their way to Leisnig. With no identity papers the chances were not in their favour but Larive had managed to smuggle paper money and a small compass out of his last POW camp into Colditz using the apple syrup trick:

> I now had to take care of my money and compass and knowing I would be subject to the most intensive search of all, it created quite a problem. I emptied a tin of apple syrup, placed the compass in the bottom of it protected by a piece of greaseproof paper and refilled the tin. The censor usually probed tins and jars with a knife to detect hidden objects and I had to think of some way to counter that. Knowing they, like anyone else, would not like to get their fingers sticky, I covered the outside of the tin with apple syrup, wrapped the tin in a very dirty piece of paper and put it right on top of everything in my suitcase.

The plan worked as the censor removed the tin from the suitcase, pulled away the paper and took the tin in his hands before noticing the syrup. He dropped it in disgust and after checking Larive's suitcase told him to pick up the tin and move along. Larive also smuggled money into Colditz using an 'arse-creeper' (an old cigar case with money or maps inside). The escape plan was to reach Leisnig in time for the first train, just after dawn. Larive's compass proved vital and the pair arrived ten minutes before departure time. Checks were almost inevitable, but there was no choice except to take the train and press on. Risks had to be minimized whatever the odds, so Steinmetz bought the tickets to Dresden as he spoke better German. Larive stood at the far end of the platform, ready to slip away if there were problems.

At Dresden, they changed trains with a plan to make for Ulm via Regensburg. Steinmetz asked the conductor for the best route and he advised they should alight at Marktredwitz where there were better connections. The town was further away from their destination and close to the border with Czechoslovakia, but with this route, they could move on to get a better train to Nuremberg and then travel direct to Ulm before going on to Singen close to the German-Swiss border. After leaving Dresden, Larive reported: 'The only scare we had from time to time was the appearance of the military police patrol. Fortunately, they seemed to confine their activities to checking military personnel.'

The train arrived at Nuremburg around midnight and there was an immediate problem. Two men hanging about a train station all night was tantamount to a confession that they were escaped prisoners. The men needed somewhere to spend the night without raising suspicion. The first train to Ulm did not depart until 6.00 am. The men had a stroke of luck: there were a surprising number of people on the streets and just off the main street, they found a church set back in total darkness. In the garden a number of benches, were occupied by courting couples making amorous noises, initially the two men felt as if they stuck out like sore thumbs but Larive quickly realized that no-one was paying them any attention. Larive led Steinmetz to a secluded bench, the blanket that was used to cover their heads when hiding at the bottom of the manhole shaft in Colditz was draped over their knees to fit as a makeshift skirt. Love-making was in steady progress all around, the intermittent sound of smacking kisses, with other noises, made the men shake with suppressed laughter. Exhaustion caught up with both Larive and Steinmetz, despite working hard on their own 'noises' to fit in. Occasionally their heads sagged down in sleep, only to wake up again with a start. Larive kept an eye out for police patrols but then a new couple came into the park from the street and carefully groped their way around in the darkness, trying to find an empty seat, they sat next to Steinmetz. The men moved on to avoid suspicion and walked slowly to the train station and arrived early enough to board a train with no security checks, they changed at Ulm and arrived in Singen station on the same day, an hour before dusk, having taken the line south-west through Ehingen and Sigmaringen. Larive remembered the territory well from his previous escape attempt. 'After handing in our tickets we left the station and turned left, right and left again, crossed the single line, turned left and came to the road running parallel to double track. I couldn't miss. I was as sure and confident as if it were my home town.'

Gottmadingen was the next destination. Larive recalled making the mistake of catching the train there on his last visit and the lessons learned from 'the Bull'. This time Larive kept to the road; as it was easier to look for landmarks the Gestapo officer had pointed out on his map, as expected the road moved into the woods. No more than half a mile to the border. From now on, the plan was to make a run for it separately if things went wrong. Unexpectedly, as the two men walked around a bend in the path they spotted a German guard post just 50 yards ahead: the situation had obviously changed since Larive's interrogation by the Gestapo. The guard spotted them and began to walk forward just as Larive and Steinmetz crossed the road, the guard began to close in and shouted 'Halt'. To the right a few yards ahead, a path led into the trees but away from the frontier, there was no choice in the matter, both men jumped into the wood and made a run for it. A shot rang out, the bullet whistling past Larive's head.

The situation was now grave. The guard did not pursue but returned to his post to raise the alarm. Gaining access to the border would now be extremely difficult. Night fell and Larive noticed that soldiers on bicycles left the guard post to take up positions on the road at about 400-yard intervals, the men needed to cross that road. Away to the right was the railway and town of Gottmadingen, the south road out of the town led to Switzerland. Larive and Steinmetz remained silent and still, observing the German patrols, out of the darkness they heard rifle shots. Larive whispered to his friend to remain believing they were shots designed to flush out the escapees, as it was unlikely the guard dogs had their scent and the rain and darkness would make searching difficult. Suddenly the men heard a search party approach and fear struck them, they continued to remain hidden, the guards passed and were heard chatting by Larive and Steinmetz but they remained undetected. Finally, at 10.00 pm, the pair crept away and, guided by their compass, they crawled painstakingly across the ground on their elbows and stomach towards the road, stopping every few yards to look and listen. Before slithering across the road, both men removed their shoes to prevent any noise. It had taken four hours to cover about 700 yards. On the run for two and a half days with just two bars of chocolate to eat, Larive and Steinmetz were hungry and exhausted from constantly feeling on edge, the tension of being so close to freedom lay in the men's innermost thoughts. Larive had been so near before. The prospect of another return to Colditz was unthinkable.

A short detour to the west before veering south again brought them to the outline of some houses. Surely, they had done enough now. Steinmetz shinned up a signpost and struck a match to get a closer look. 'Deutsche Zollant' – German Customs. Of all the signposts to shin up! They ran away expecting to hear angry German guards about to challenge them but they managed to keep moving for 15 minutes when the saw a small group of houses. Were they Swiss or German? Larive's navigation led him to believe they were now in Switzerland, soaked through, cold and very hungry Larive struggled to concentrate. Then suddenly the stinging white beam of a strong torch flashed on them and the German words '*Wer sind Sie? Was Machen Sie hier?*' (Who are you? What are you doing here?). Larive was furious, violent anger overpowered him and he began to feel tears come to his eyes: 'caught again, a hundred yards, maybe fifty yards from the border.' Each man had agreed that if they were this close they would attack to cross the border. They were ready to launch themselves at the guard when he spoke again in German. '*Sie sind in der Schweiz. Sie mussen mit mir kommen!*' (You are in Switzerland. You'll have to come with me.)

Hans Larive provided the intelligence which established the Singen Route, a pathway to Switzerland other escapees from Colditz used to gain freedom. Returning to active service Larive was appointed the Senior Dutch Officer of Motor Torpedo Boats of the Netherlands and after the war worked for the Royal Dutch Shell company. Hans Larive died in the Hague in 1984.

Major Cornelis Giebel and 2nd Lieutenant Oscar Drijber – Netherlands

Sunday, 31 August 1941 happened to be the birthday of the Queen of Netherlands and the Dutch officers were keen to hold a service in her honour. Permission was given by the Kommandant but the fellow prisoners kicked up a stink as it clashed with the opening ceremony of the International Sports competition, or 'the Colditz Olympics' as it was dubbed. After three weeks of competition the closing ceremony was due to take place at 10:30 am on 21 September but the German guards held an *Appel* and realized two Dutch officers were missing. Saturday, 20 September was the revised date for Dutchmen Major Cornelis Giebel and 2nd Lieutenant Oscar Drijber to attempt their escape. They planned to leave on the Friday using the manhole trick in the exercise paddock, but there had been a problem at the Castle around the daily park exercise. Giebel recorded:

Drijber and I joined the others of the walk party in front of the closed doors at the gateway. We were however quite amazed to see this time the walk party numbered more than twice its usual number. Instead of about eighty, there were now some two hundred. When the doors were opened, we pushed our way through to the outer courtyard where our thirty German guards were waiting for us …But things went wrong. Was it only accidental that Captain Priem was on the spot? Confronted with two hundred park walkers instead of the usual eighty, he at once understood that something was brewing. But he knew how to handle the situation. With an ironic smile he addressed the POW crowd, apologising that apparently it had not become known in time that on this Friday the walk in the park had been cancelled. He regretted that we had not been warned earlier and suggested that we should forthwith retire behind the walls of our inner courtyard.

We could do nothing but obey. Back in the quarters we learned that our escape committee had urged some of our fellow prisoners to take part in the walk that Friday because they might be needed for camouflage purposes. But it had been overdone a little bit. The committee had underestimated everyone's desire to be helpful.

The plan was a repeat of the Larive escape using the manhole in the exercise paddock. However, the guards had grown wise to this weakness and inserted a heavy metal bolt. Unperturbed, van Doorninck held Bible classes in large numbers around the manhole whilst a pair of spanners belonging to Captain Machiel van den Heuvel (the Dutch Escape Officer), manufactured from metal bedframes, prized the bolt from its clasp. In an ingenious design van den Heuvel had a replacement bolt and nuts made of glass and wood painted, when the guards inspected it, nothing would appear suspicious. Major Giebel and Lieutenant Drijber would take the real bolt with them into the manhole and smash their way out, the glass and wood replacement shattered, and once out the men fastened the real bolt back into place. On the 20th a key football match in the 'Olympic Games' was to be played in the park between the Polish and Dutch teams. Both teams and their supporters assembled with other POWs in the courtyard for the count and march down to the park. The Feldwebel in charge referred to recent instructions and refused to allow Dutch supporters to accompany their team to the park. The Dutch players protested, complaining that they could not play the match without supporters. During the impasse, one of the Polish prisoners accused the Feldwebel of going against the Kommandant's personal wishes, which stated that the inmates should be allowed to play the 'Olympic Games' amongst themselves. The Feldwebel eventually conceded, and the prisoners lined up to be counted. The escape was on.

There were several challenges which were requiring attention if the escape was to be successful. In ordinary circumstances prisoners could camouflage the manhole with rugby or Bible readings, but on this occasion the manhole cover was actually within the marked-out pitch. In addition, the absence of two prisoners had to be covered when the count was made on return to the Castle. Firstly, two of the smallest Poles in the camp had positioned themselves amongst the lines of Dutch supporters. Each man clamped his legs around a fellow POW's thighs whilst someone either side supported him by the elbows. The man in the middle wrapped his overcoat and some blankets around the hidden POW and was able to open a newspaper to complete the deception. If Giebel and Drijber managed to get into the hole unseen these Poles would 'appear' for the count, if not they would be taken back to the Castle as they were brought down to the park.

Initially it is difficult to understand why this ruse was not spotted. Prisoners were lined up in rows and a diligent guard would surely detect the concealed men. The reality was not that straightforward. The two Poles were very small, and men often lined up in a haphazard, testing way, pushing each other and their luck as far as they could stretch it. Goon-baiting was also the equivalent of a national sport inside the Castle, especially at *Appel*. Hauptmann Eggers gives an accurate picture of what the Germans had to contend with around the congregation and line up for the park exercise:

First the assembly, stage one, getting the party out of the yard. Then stage two, falling them in, in five ranks, for the count outside the guardroom. No one was ever in a hurry. People stood around chatting. '*Zu funf, meine Herren,*' bawled our NCO in charge. No one moved. 'Guard turn out'. Those for the walk eventually started to line up, in fives. Gradually the prisoners drifted into ranks, 'close up here, cover off there' and then the count. Someone moved, someone shuffled, someone dropped his football, someone had to be shouted out of his book. Perhaps a recount was necessary, and then another one, and finally the total was written down …

Giebel and Drijber entered the park enclosure with the other POWs. The headcount had agreed with numbers leaving the Castle earlier. There must have been a tentative rush of optimism. If they were able to hide in the manhole shaft, the two Polish POWs could easily take their place in the counts taken before exit from the park and back at the Castle entrance. However, the glass bolt and wooden nut had to be removed to give Giebel and Drijber access to the manhole and replaced with a false one without the guards seeing. This time Giebel and Drijber had to make best use of the football match and spectators. Giebel described what happened once the match was in progress:

> The Dutch supporters seemed to be not content with the place where they were standing, which was muddy, so we moved forward a few feet across the touchline in the direction of the manhole. When a few minutes later we moved forward again, the players objected and said we were spoiling their game and should keep off the field. But that did not stop us from moving step by step, nearer to the manhole.

A screen formed around the manhole again and work began with the home-made spanners to remove the nut and bolt. Whoever screwed on the nut last had done a thorough job. It was hard to remove; work had to be done intermittently and discreetly. The spanners would remain on the floor next to the bolt and different prisoners would bend down appearing to re-tie a lace or retrieve something dropped to the ground, turn the bolt slowly and stand upright to view the game again. It was slow progress but the delicacy of the operation called for a subtle approach with guards circling the football pitch.

With ten minutes of the game remaining the manhole cover was opened. Giebel and Drijber climbed down the rungs to the bottom of the shaft and the false bolt and nut were cosmetically secured in position without the guards noticing. It was a masterstroke, as the grey paint on the carved wooden bolt and glass tube which had once contained aspirin looked authentic. Giebel and Drijber entered the manhole on the 19th but were not identified as missing until the 21st just before the closing ceremony was about to begin. Two precious days' head start. This was orchestrated by Captain van den Heuvel and 'Max' and 'Moritz', two recent arrivals at Colditz. Van den Heuvel had managed to acquire a sack of ceiling plaster by bribing a workman in the Castle and in most POW camps there was usually a raft of trades and talents amongst the prisoners. A sculptor fashioned two life-sized busts which were then painted by Lieutenant Diederick van Lyden. Two iron hoops were added around the pedestal part of the bust which was then shaped to rest on a man's arm. A shirt collar and tie were fitted around the neck and a long Dutch overcoat draped over the bust's shoulders. Another neat twist was when not being shown, the bust hung suspended under the forearm of the handler, hidden in the folds of the overcoat. To an observer it looked like the POW was carrying the coat on his arm. When the bust needed to stand in at a head count, the handler unfolded the overcoat, raised the dummy up and put an army cap on its head. The impostor was then held at shoulder height by a shortened broomstick pushed through the hole in the bust's neck. The handler kept his arm at elbow height, concealing it amongst the overcoat. A pair of high military boots were placed at attention under the bottom of the coat by another prisoner.

Somewhere amongst the rows of men at evening *Appel* 'Max', 'Moritz' and their handlers did the job to perfection. Giebel and Drijber waited until it was dark, pushed up the manhole cover, breaking the glass 'bolt' and making their escape after gathering up the shards of glass. 'Max' and 'Moritz' covered five more *Appels* before van den Heuvel dropped the ruse and allowed the missing numbers to be discovered. By then Giebel and Drijber had a 36-hour start and were well on their way to the Swiss frontier. Which was safely crossed on 23 September 1941. Whilst Giebel and Drijber were being held by the neutral Swiss authorities in Berne, they were able to write an innocent-looking letter which was coded and contained detailed intelligence around their escape. They also included a false chessboard and pieces which contained smuggled contraband including German banknotes, maps and intelligence. The package was wrapped in a Dutch newspaper, *Vry Neduland*, that was printed in London and contained an article on Queen

Wilhelmina and her radio broadcast to her people in occupied Holland. The letter reached the POWs in Colditz, was decoded and assisted future escapes.

On 24 November a sentry spotted two men, Lieutenant Wardle and Wojciechowski, unscrewing the bolt and dropping into the manhole out of sight. Finally, Eggers had located the Dutch route of escape. The manhole had iron bars placed across it the very next day.

Lieutenant Francis Steinmetz – Netherlands

Francis Steinmetz was born in the Dutch East Indies on 20 September 1914 and entered the Dutch Royal Navy aged 18 in September 1932. Captured in Amsterdam by the swift advancing German forces, Steinmetz was requested to sign a cessation of hostilities document by the Gestapo. As a Jewish man Steinmetz ran a considerable risk when he refused to sign and was immediately transferred to a camp at Soest and later Colditz when he explained to his captors that not only would he continue to fight against Nazi tyranny he would be making regular escapes! Throughout the summer of 1941, the escape season was in full swing, Steinmetz began plotting with his fellow Dutchmen of a way to escape the confines of the Castle. The 'man hole' escape was a well-rehearsed method of escape and courtesy of Larive's previous escape and recapture the men knew they could reach the Swiss border via the Singen Route. On 15 August 1941 Steinmetz and Hans Larive hid under a drain cover in the exercise field shadowed by a ferocious maul in a game of rugby accompanied by much complaining and a halt in play as men slowly rose to their feet to cover the activity. Lieutenant Gerrit Dames then created a diversion by cutting a hole in the barbed wire fence, before allowing himself to be caught, facing away from the Castle he shouted to imaginary officers to run, so that the Germans would believe he was the third man, with two already away.

Duly, the guards set off at a pace into the trees to search for escapers whilst a *Sonderappell* (special *Appel*) identified Larive and Steinmetz as absent. Guards tore through the Dutch quarters and located items of civilian clothing and a map with instructions of how to travel from Tuttlingen in South-West Germany and get across the Swiss frontier. This was a significant find. The

Germans would need every scrap of information. The *Sonderappel* had revealed three more Dutch officers, Lieutenants Kruimink, van der Krap and van Lynden were also missing. Hours passed with no sign of the missing men, searches were conducted of the surrounding area with the help of police and the Hitler Youth. Intelligence gathered from bribing guards told the officers that the protocol after the alarm was raised followed four key steps. 1) Search parties sent out on foot to cover the immediate neighbourhood and watch local roads. 2) A group on bicycles spreading out in a larger area to operate in a similar way. 3) Railway and police stations in the area alerted. Once the prisoner's identity was known, police in Leipzig were also notified. They had photographs and descriptions of the prisoners on file. Leipzig was a railway junction that escaped prisoners may attempt to travel through. 4) If there were no immediate results, the search would be quickly widened with all known information. The men were aware that if they could remain hidden, it was possible that the Germans would suspect they had already left the area by train. In the manhole Steinmetz and Larive were having difficulty holding the blanket above their heads for long periods in the pitch black. The lower metre of the hole was filled with rainwater which was cold and numbed their legs. Around 10.00 pm Larive and Steinmetz exited the shaft, climbed over the wire fence surrounding the enclosure and scaled the 12ft park perimeter wall by climbing a nearby tree. Negotiating barbed wire on top of the wall with the aid of the blanket, they landed safely on the other side and began the three hour walk to the small town of Leisnig.

Steinmetz felt apprehension at the thought of leaving the sheltered known world of the POW camp, but that quickly passed and was replaced by joy – they had done it. The small-town railway station had no guard and despite having no identity papers or travel permits arriving in the early morning after lying low the men caught a train and sat quietly in the carriage, each man occupied with his own thoughts. Travel on the faster routes had been their preferred choice, despite the increased risk of checks on identity and travel papers. At Dresden, they changed trains with a plan to make for Ulm via Regensburg. Steinmetz asked the conductor for the best route and he advised they should travel to Marktredwitz where there were better connections. The town was further away from their destination and close to the border with Czechoslovakia, but with this route, they could move on to get a better train to Nurnberg and then travel direct to Ulm before going on to Singen close to the German-Swiss border. Singen was the last station before stringent checks near the Swiss border, Larive had been detained just a few miles from the border on a previous breakout and his interrogation by an errant Gestapo officer became a lesson in how to improve escaping. Larive was told how to move from Singen through to the unguarded section of the Swiss border on a map and how he had walked past part of the Swiss border which jutted into Germany at a distance of only about 300 yards. He asked numerous questions 'which could be of any interest to an escaper and learned a lot.' The biggest coup was ascertaining that there was no real defence line on the border with Switzerland and he could have walked across. If they could reach Singen, they stood a good chance of making it safely to Switzerland.

On the train the men were relieved to discover that patrols of the carriages concentrated on military personnel and neither man was asked for papers. The train arrived at Nurnberg around midnight and Steimetz and Larive discovered an immediate problem, their connecting train to Ulm did not depart until 06.00 hours and stations and waiting rooms were regularly checked after midnight for obvious reasons. The men faced the ordeal of leaving a railway station for over five hours with no idea where they were going, in a city they did not know with the threat of discovery. They would have to leave immediately and keep well away until at least 05.30. To avoid suspicion they decided to walk a circular route near to the station so they could keep an eye on any military personal and the path they chose was dark because of the black out and had no checkpoints. Out of the darkness Larive and Steinmetz whispered over their next movements and decided to take cover in a nearby graveyard with the blanket wrapped around them to stave off the cold and rain. Dressed in light civilian clothing, no coats and only a few bars of chocolate in their stomachs the identity of the two men remained a secret from others in the park, mostly courting couples. After a while the men had no choice but to join in the amorous noises emanating from behind a gravestone a few feet away for fear of arousing suspicion. Steinmetz used the blanket as a makeshift skirt and Larive began smacking his lips against his arm to replicate passionate kissing. It was 3.00 am before the couple next door had finished and left the graveyard, at last both men could relax. The importance of the cover of trees and bushes was crucial for the men, as they arrived at the train station just after 5:30 am, appearing dry and ready for a normal day, to board their train. A Polish officer had warned them that the Gestapo patrol train stations but there was no military presence, Larive and Steinmetz boarded the train without issue.

The following evening the men had made safe passage through to Singen, departed the train station and began to follow 'the Bull's' advice (the Gestapo officer who had schooled Larive in his errors of his last escape). They found the railway line which led south-west to Switzerland, the same one which carried Alain Le Ray to freedom some months before to a first 'home run'. As expected, a road appeared which crossed the line and moved down away to the frontier, the men followed it and expected to see the Ramsen saliant a hundred yards ahead of them. Suddenly, an armed patrol appeared into view, a hundred yards away, Larive and Steinmetz exchanged glances, 'the Bull' was wrong! Larive and Steinmetz crossed the road, the guard followed and moved toward them, unshouldering his rifle, they had come so close, the anger of being caught again so close to the border was immense. Without consulting each other, the men broke for the woods, gunshot rang out and missed, the guard doubled back to the guard house 400 yards away to raise the alarm; Steinmetz and Larive found a thicket of bushes and covered themselves in leaves and moss. The pair heard rifle shots somewhere behind them and barking dogs. Run or stay? It was best to remain hidden. A risk, but it was unlikely the dogs had their scent and the rain and darkness would make searching difficult. The rifle fire was an effort to flush the men out and for the dogs to latch on to the sound of them running away. The search party came close, but finally moved onto the nearby village of Gottmadingen. Around ten o'clock Larive and Steinmetz observed that just one sentry remained, they watched him for nearly 15 minutes wondering where it was safe to make a dash for the border. The sentry turned out to be a tree! Removing their shoes the men folded up their blanket and slithered away, guided by a compass, they crawled painstakingly across the ground on their elbows and stomach towards the road, stopping every few yards to look and listen. A short detour to the west before veering south again brought them to the outline of some houses. Surely they had done enough now. Steinmetz shinned up a signpost and struck a match to get a closer look. 'Deutsche Zollant' – German Customs. They ran away expecting the shots which never came. It had taken 4 hours to cover about 650 yards when they stumbled upon a dirt track which they followed into a valley, there was no sound and the blackness of night made navigation difficult. Under an overhanging roof of a shed the men discussed their predicament in whispers, should they remain where they were believing they had crossed the border, or move on and risk confusion and possibly slipping back into Germany by mistake. Steinmetz and Larive had spent three nights outside and were half dozing when a light was shone in their eyes and then heard what they feared to hear most of all – German: *'Wer sind Sie? Was Machen Sie hier?'* (Who are you? What are you doing here?) Each man had the same thought, they were prepared to attack and just before they launched themselves toward the guard Steinmetz caught a glimpse of the white cross on a red circle, a Swiss guard insignia. The men were in Switzerland.

In German Steinmetz said *'Wir sind Hollander'* (We are Dutch) and the guard replied, 'You must come with me, you are in Switzerland'. The Dutch recorded seven 'Home Runs', a remarkable total when the prisoners of war from Holland only occupied Colditz for a short period before being taken to Stalag 371 in Stanislau to join their countrymen. Larive and Steinmetz were the first of the seven from the Netherlands to escape. In Geneva the men were debriefed and it was explained that under Swiss neutrality law they were not permitted to leave the country, the Dutch Legation stepped in and provided false papers where they were employed as 'sugar planters' on their way to Cuba. They travelled on a sealed train in which neutrals were able to pass through France into Spain, this enabled the men to board the neutral ship, *Isla de Teneriffe*, at Barcelona sailing for Havana. The ship was intercepted by a Royal Navy cutter in the Strait of Gibraltar and the two men were released and then sailed to England aboard the submarine HNLMS *O 21* and arrived in London on 17 December 1941. At the Patriotic School of London they were debriefed again and were granted an audience with Queen Wilhelmina who was visibly moved when Steinmetz explained the patriotic fervour and loyalty of the Dutchmen who refused to sign Hitler's Declaration inside the walls of Colditz.

Steinmetz served for the remainder of the war on motor torpedo boats, taking *MTB 222* to the West Indies. He later commanded Dutch motor torpedo boats in the Far East. After the end of hostilities, Steinmetz returned to Holland and served at the naval training camp at Hilversum. Steinmetz later commanded the minesweeper *De Bitter* and the frigate *De Zeeuw*, before joining the Dutch Ministry of Naval Affairs. His final ship was the destroyer *Limburg*. The guards in Colditz could not explain how Steinmetz and Larive had escaped from the Castle, but four months later they realized when a British–Polish escape was uncovered by a guard witnessing two men slip into the drain.

Canadian Escapes

Flight Lieutenant Howard (Hank) Wardle – Canada

Howard Wardle was born in Manitoba, Canada on 14 August 1915 and worked as a bookkeeper. With war looming Hank and two friends set sail for England to join the RAF, but only Hank was successful. In March 1939, Hank was granted a Short Service Commission. After completing his training and gaining his wings, he was posted to No.98 Bomber Squadron based at RAF Hucknall in November 1939. This stay was short lived, as on November 29, he, along with his observer Sergeant Edward Davidson and air gunner Aircraftman 1 Class Albert Bailey, were posted to No.218 Bomber Squadron in Auberive-sur-Suippes, France. On Saturday, 20 April 1940, the squadron was instructed to make ready four aircraft and crew, their mission that night to carry out a reconnaissance of the Rhine and 'Nickle drop' (the codename for dropping propaganda leaflets across Germany) over the towns of Darmstadt and Mainz.

While over Germany Hank's Fairey Battle came under fire from Feldwebel Schmale of the 12th Staffel JG2 at 12.45 am. A fire broke out on board, Wardle ordered the crew to bail out, but only he survived. This encounter is reported to be the first instance of a British bomber being shot down over Germany at night. Wardle was picked up by a local policeman and interrogated before being sent to Spangenburg Prison from where he attempted his first escape in August 1940 by leaping from a window in the gymnasium and down several terraces and through barbed wire. Whilst at a railway crossing Wardle was stopped by a patrol and arrested. As a result of this escape he was despatched to Oflag VI-C Colditz. In Colditz he was involved in various tunnel schemes and in the spring of 1941 Wardle was one of thirteen men caught in a tunnel as they broke ground to escape the Castle. This attempt was organized before the Escape Committees developed international relations within Colditz. The French were sawing at iron bars just above the tunnel and a sentry was alerted by the noise only to stumble on the shovel as it broke through the grass on a verge.

Major Littledale and Lieutenant Commander Stephens gained permission from the Escape Committee for an escape through the kitchens, into the outer courtyard across the flat roof of a boiler house but no other details were finalized! The plan to cross the flat roofs did give the prisoners access to a carpenter's cellar during the escape, from which a narrow flue led to the outside terrace, once the men descended each terrace a road led past the married quarters to a wall which could easily be scaled. The plan required a skilled lockpicker so Major Pat Reid was enlisted, and Hank made up the party of four. Reid and Wardle moved across the inner courtyard during the evening of 14 October 1942, progressed through a kitchen window and overlooked the outer courtyard. The bar had been removed and replaced with false a one which slipped out, the men then proceeded onto the flat roof and dropped 10ft to the ground. The men stood silently in a darkened doorway waiting for Littledale and Stephens to join them but there was a failure in the signalling system which involved playing an accordion from the upper quarters. The men could hear nothing and waited silently for over two hours. Finally, the men decided to wait until the sentry's back was turned to move down the terrace, suddenly the guard turned abruptly and Reid and Wardle fell to the floor. Reid had not moved far enough down the terrace and the sentry was walking right toward him, in the dim light the guard strode less than a metre from the prisoner, turned and began walking back toward the far end of the terrace. Wardle and Reid reached the carpenter's cellar with no further incident and rested, waiting for Littledale and Stephens who arrived shortly after.

Each man passed successfully through the flue to the outer castle, an Alsatian barked furiously as the men moved toward the wall past the married quarters but no alert was raised. The men scaled the outer wall and parted at 4.00 am: their escape from the inner courtyard had taken seven hours. Reid and Wardle wished the other men luck and began walking south-east until first light when they sheltered in the undergrowth of woodland. Through 15 and 16 October the two men crossed the River Hulde and having washed and shaved as best they could they caught a train from Penig to Zwickau.

As Wardle and Reid moved further away from the Castle they relaxed into their roles as civilians more, showing the same frustration as those sharing the waiting room at a train station when an air raid delayed their train to Munich by two hours. Wardle explained in his escape report that the men enjoyed a coupon-free meal at Munich station, potato and vegetable soup, the irony that Hitler was feeding prisoners in the midst of an escape not being lost on Wardle. Whilst following Hans Larrive's safe Singen route toward the Swiss border Wardle encountered some difficulties when they left Tuttlingen station and began their walk to freedom on 18 October. Upon arriving Reid and Wardle took a road heading south-east which led them to a heavily camouflaged factory in the early morning. Immediately retreating the men had had a narrow escape as the guards had not seen them. The men moved across country using a brass button compass to navigate. A forester observed them through the woodland whilst he ate his lunch, Wardle and Reid moved quickly to outrun him. As they crossed the open hills between Hilzingen and Singen a cycle patrol stopped them on a small track and demanded an explanation as well as their identity papers: these were satisfactorily given. Once out of sight of the sentry Wardle describes moving west along the country track, along the tree line of woods and they crossed a double track railway which brought them to the Singen-Gottmadingen road at 6.00 pm. Remaining at the side of the road until a period when traffic was light, they crossed the road quietly and hid in bushes on the other side. Wardle then explained in his report how they moved toward Ramsden under the cover of evening darkness, with the moon smothered by clouds. At 8.00 pm Reid and Wardle walked into the village of Ramsen, Switzerland as free men and gave themselves up in the local police station.

Wardle remained in neutral Switzerland for almost a year, as finding a safe route to Britain, including a secure route to a port with secluded safe houses and guides, was not a simple task. A Dutch-Paris escape line was established by Edmond 'Moen' Chait which initially held the purpose of transporting Jews from Holland and Belgium through France to Spain to board ships for Britain. A British military attache made the arrangements (Wardle was issued with a fake passport in the name of Raoul, Hank was now a hairdresser) and supplied the money for Wardle to pass through occupied France with a party of two Italian deserters, three Frenchmen and seven

Dutchmen under the guidance of two French guides, Henri Marot known as Mireille and Pierre 'Palo' Treillet. Travelling in December 1943 across the Pyrenees to avoid detection was a hard task with heavy snow and strong winds across the mountains, Wardle crossed the mountains with an injured leg, the result of a severe beating he had received when captured after his first escape attempt in 1940. While in Oflag IV-C he often walked with the aid of a walking stick, and he was also partially deaf in one ear, the result of a blow from a rifle butt. Wardle was exhausted when the group reached the small Spanish village of Canejan on 22 December 1943. From Gibraltar, he reached the United Kingdom on 5 February 1944.

In 1944 he married June Porter and began ferrying bombers to the Middle and Far East. Hank was awarded the Military Cross – awarded as per the *London Gazette* dated 16 May 1944. Towards the end of the war, he still ferrying bombers, switched to flying bombers from Canada across the Atlantic to the United Kingdom. Hank died in 1995 in Ottawa, Canada at the age of 80.

Lieutenant William Anderson Millar – Canada

On 2 March 1944 Heinrich Himmler authorized a document known as 'Aktion K', translated as Action Kugel (Bullet) which stated any escaped prisoners of war that were not used for 'essential war work' would be taken to Mauthausen. Upon arrival at this camp, prisoners marked with a 'K' on their papers would be separated from the rest, executed and their bodies immediately burned. The only exception were Anglo-American soldiers who would have their cases judged on individual merit. Lieutenant William Millar disappeared on his escape from Colditz. There are two possibilities for his fate. It is believed that William Millar was captured near Lamsdorf in the summer of 1941 and executed by the Gestapo at Mauthausen shortly after or he escaped through Czechoslovakia and made a home run.

Lieutenant William Millar was born in 1913 in Canada, the eldest of a family of four boys, he was a member of the local Militia (1934–6) and became a Corporal in Artillery Survey. Whilst studying Engineering and Mining Engineering at the University of Alberta he became a member of the Canadian Officer Training Corps. Upon graduating in 1938 he began his civilian career with mining companies in British Columbia, Saskatchewan and Northern Ontario. Millar was working with Canadian Industries Limited in Montreal as a mining engineer and explosives expert with a specialty in tunnelling and special demolition techniques for underground excavations when he enlisted for service in the Second World War in 1941. After completing his military and field engineering training at Camp Petawawa, he embarked for the UK in November 1941 as a Reinforcement Officer. In April 1942 he was selected as one of the Team Leaders for Operation Rutter, the codename for the raid on Dieppe which was scheduled for between 4 and 8 July until some very poor weather prevented the convoy from sailing. In addition German pilots reported the presence of vessels in the Solent and attempted to bomb the convoy. Little damage was done but the Germans became evidently aware an amphibious landing may be planned. Operation Rutter became Operation Jubilee on 18/19 August. Millar commanded a party of fifty-five all ranks for the operation that was to land on Red Beach. His party was organized into four groups and their tasks after clearing the immediate beach obstacles during the assault phase were to demolish a number of assigned cranes and warehouses in the Dieppe dock area, co-ordinate activities with Navy cutting-out force, and to liaise with the Essex Scottish Regiment. On the morning of 19 August 1942, Millar and his team landed on Red Beach. Their landing was conducted under extreme combat conditions as the Germans had prepared many fields of fire intended to stop landing craft and advancing forces. Under fire, the team began their tasks of destroying and demolishing beach obstacles and attempted to advance to their demolition targets. However, as with many of the landed troops, they were prevented from advancing from the beach because of the intense fire from German small arms, heavy machine guns, mortars, anti-tank guns and field artillery sited around the cliffs and beaches of Dieppe.

Lieutenant Millar was witnessed during the assault to be leading his team to safety, administering to their wounds and to be directing their defence, while still attempting to continue to advance over Red Beach towards his assigned demolition targets. Most of his team, however, had drowned in the surf labouring with their heavy loads, had been killed outright, or had suffered serious wounds. Despite his best efforts, he was unable to get the survivors to safety and the team, including Millar, was captured, and taken prisoner of war. They were then shipped by train under guard to a designated officer POW camp in Eichstatt. Enroute to the camp, Millar escaped from the train but was quickly recaptured and sent under heavier guard to Eichstatt and transferred later to Willisbad (Prison) Castle. Millar escaped from Willisbad Castle after three days but was recaptured several miles away. He was subsequently sent back to the officer POW camp at Eichstatt. Unperturbed, Millar joined a team of British prisoners working on an escape tunnel and Millar's engineering experience proved invaluable for ensuring the integrity of the passage. Many men escaped, including Millar, but he was caught in Austria and suffered the humiliation of returning to Willisbad Castle, and then to Eichstatt. At this stage, Millar was designated as a 'persistent escaper' and transferred to the highest security POW prison at Colditz Castle.

Upon arrival Millar, Major Gordon Rolfe and Douggie Moir joined forces to hatch a plan using a length of cord smuggled into the Schloss and slipping down from a common room window when the sentry was distracted. Rolfe had two window bars replaced and Moir exited first, with Rolfe second and Millar replacing the 'iron' bar before bringing up the rear. They hung in mid-air watching the sentry below pace up and down along the grass verge. Just as Rolfe and Moir were about to touch the grass a sentry spotted them and raised the alarm. All were detained in solitary confinement. Unperturbed, Millar escaped from Colditz on 28 January 1944 by exploiting an air raid which plunged the Castle into darkness with a covering siren drowning out any noise as he slipped across the courtyard and latched on to the underside of a German truck. The truck drove out of the Castle shortly after with Millar clinging to its underside, that was the last time his friends in Colditz saw him alive.

Millar had contacts in Prague just 100 miles away and he may have reached the safe house only to be arrested enroute toward Russian territory. Another theory was that Millar was recaptured two weeks later near Lamsdorf and taken to the camp at Stalag VIIIB. Removed and taken under heavy guard by the German Secret Police to the Mauthausen Concentration Camp in Austria. He may have been shot dead under the 'Aktion K' decree on 15 July

1944 with his body being cremated and his ashes scattered amongst those of other murdered camp inmates.

Lieutenant William Millar is remembered for his tenacity of spirit and enduring desire to defeat the Nazi forces of evil. Millar was awarded a 'Mention in Dispatches' for his actions and leadership under extreme combat conditions on Red Beach at Dieppe. Awarded posthumously on 15 June 1946, this recognition was originally submitted as a Military Cross, but that award could not be made posthumously. That proposed MC citation concluded with: '…Among prisoners who had shown great determination, ingenuity, skill and daring in many and varied attempts to escape, there were few who could equal Lieutenant Millar's record of four successful breaks in a period of seventeen months, and none who surpassed him in determination and daring. Such extraordinary resolution and courage are deserving of the highest commendation.'

Millar's name is entered on the Canadian memorial in the Canadian Dieppe Cemetery, on the University of Alberta War Memorial, and Brookwood Memorial in the Brookwood Military Cemetery near London.

French Escapes

Lieutenant Jacques Durand-Hornus – France

At the end of 1941 Reinhold Eggers presented the camp Kommandant Colonel Schmidt with a document containing the following figures:

	British	French	Belgian	Polish	Dutch
Number of tries to getaway	25	30	6	19	14
Caught inside camp	23	6	6	10	8
Caught outside camp	2	14	0	8	2
Home runs	0	10	0	1	4

The French led the way with ten home runs followed by a very strong showing from the Dutch contingent. The prisoners from these two nations held an advantage on their English counterparts as if they could reach the French or Dutch border they could rely on relatives and friends to aid their disappearance. Nonetheless, the English were very disappointed with their efforts when Christmas arrived in 1941. Colonel Schmidt was very experienced. In his late 60s, he struck an imposing figure. Confirming the idea of a Prussian colonel, he often made a snap inspection through the camp: security, mail control, administration. Schmidt was tough on any officers who attempted escape but despite this he never violated international law. He rarely used to the full his power to punish his prisoners. When, near the end of his time in 1942, their behaviour verged on mutiny, he did not employ force to restore military authority in the camp, preferring court martial as a weapon. Nevertheless, when an escape failed Scmidt took great interest in the method and location of the attempt.

This meant escape became more difficult as Schmidt worked hard to close the weak area,.

Despite the cold winter weather and tight security the French determination to escape saw an advantage loom in mid-December as Eggers was on a month's leave and the atmosphere around the Castle was relaxed. In the cold winter it was thought that the prisoners would think less of an escape attempt. On 17 December 1941 the guards were having a Christmas meal led by Egger's deputy, Oberstleutnant von Kirchbach, who had lost an arm in the First World War and was far from a stickler for discipline. Under the relaxed environment von Kirchbach allowed any dental work beyond the simple fillings to be done at the town dentist. On this particular occasion the French prison officer dentist did not have the required materials to treat Durand-Hornus and he, along with six others, were sent to the town dentist on a foggy afternoon, which was a gift to the committed escaper. Upon leaving the dentist the guard was at the rear and as Durand-Hornus, Prot and de Frondville moved outside they simply scarpered in different directions. The guard was at a loss, unable to follow all three and he could not risk opening fire in such foggy weather. Fluent in French and English and armed with excellent false papers Durand-Hornus vanished. No trace of him was found and he returned to France within a week, surviving the war and recording the thirteenth 'home run' for the prisoners and the eighth for France.

Lieutenant Alain Le Ray – France

Night after night I did my shift with the tunnel team. And I was happy to do it, to keep solidarity with my mates, but it was very hard work and frustrating because progress was so slow. Who knows if it could survive without being discovered. I knew tunnelling did not suit me, I was too important.

On 11 April 1941 Lieutenant Alain Le Ray became a free man for the first time since his capture and incarceration in Oflag IV-C. He was also the first man to escape from Colditz Castle. Born on 3 October 1910, Le Ray joined the French Army from military college before moving to the Chasseurs

Alpins, the elite army mountain troops (he was a skilled mountaineer). Le Ray was taken captive in June 1940 and sent to Colditz after a failed escape. Colditz at that time was a place of relative calm as Red Cross parcels arrived regularly and the evacuation at Dunkirk had left the British fighting the Nazi blitzkrieg alone. With winter in 1940 approaching there seemed an uneasy truce with no possibility of invasion across the English Channel prisoners and guards chatted and even enjoyed some alcohol which had been sent into the Castle. Eggers made sure that this was rationed. The Poles even put on a marionette show with musical accompaniments and a translated commentary. *Snow White and Seven Dwarfs* was the main event with a history of Poland and ending with the national anthem, the Dombrowska March. Eggers wrote in his 'school report' that the Poles were top in morale, the French were still licking their wounds after a humiliating defeat and the British, as the new boys, were still settling in, although he suspected they were working on a large-scale tunnel under the canteen floor. After Christmas 1940 the prisoners really set to work with thirteen of the thirty-one official escapes coming in one calendar year, Eggers' prediction of having all the naughty boys in one place became a reality.

Le Ray wanted a quick escape. The prisoners exercised in an enclosure at the end of a 'windy' track under close guard. (Scrutinized closely at the end of a meandering track prisoners had their daily exercise, glad to stretch their legs and take in some different scenery, they paid little attention to the overbearing guards.) The men were marched under close guard down the track, but they were not counted. On a sharp bend in the track was a deserted Terrace House in derelict condition, Le Ray felt he could dash up the bank to the door and force it open or slip around the side of the building. It was a risk as the guard could be as close as ten yards away, but Le Ray calculated the bend was sharp enough to conceal his movement. Before the war Le Ray has visited the Colditz area and drew a map from memory, which was used by fellow prisoners on later escapes. Provided with some German marks and civilian clothes the French commanding officer offered the parting words, 'Bon voyage' and Le Ray joined the other prisoners on the march toward the exercise yard dressed in a greatcoat with civilian clothes underneath. As the prisoners played football Le Ray considered the possibility of success. The men lined up at the end of the allotted time and marched up, under guard, toward the Castle. Le Ray approached the bend and causally glanced behind him, the guard was ten feet away but looking down at the path. Le Ray seized his chance, whipped his greatcoat off and handed it to a fellow officer and scrambled up the bank toward the house and slid behind the front door. There were no shouts or cheers, the party moved up the path slowly and gradually disappeared out of sight, Le Ray was alone. 'I was sure they would see me, but there were no shots, no chase, no dogs.'

Quickly, Le Ray moved down toward the park. He felt exposed, describing as if the whole park was like a great eye watching him, then he scaled the perimeter wall to breathe free air. Walking five miles Le Ray was undisturbed and wandered into the town of Rochlitz where he bordered a train for Penig. Eggers organized a snap *Appel* with photographs of each man only to find that many images were a year old and, true to form, the prisoners had grown all manner of beards, moustaches and some homemade haircuts left them virtually unrecognizable. The natural excitement and standard chaos which the inmates brought to the process also helped buy Le Ray more time. General Kommando Dresden and their Abwehrstelle 4 Security department demanded to know how the French officer had escaped, 'When did the prisoner escape? How did he get out? What clothes did he wear?' The guards at Colditz did not know any of these answers. The Oberkommando der Werrmacht in Berlin wanted to know which officer was responsible for the lapse in security and whether punishment had been meted out. Colditz Castle was in disgrace at this breach of its walls and the national security risk. New rules were imposed on Colditz staff for the humiliation: pay closer attention to duties, no drinking after midnight and lights out at 1.00 am.

Le Ray planned to travel by train to a neutral country but soon ran into difficulties as his currency card was invalid, being out of date. At Penig Le Ray hid in a guard's room next to the train station, he jumped on a train which took him to Nuremburg where he ran out of funds. Freezing and desperate Le Ray hid in an alleyway and watched as a man slowly walked toward him in the mist of the night. As the man drew close to him Le Ray leapt from the shadows and gave the unsuspecting civilian two hard punches to the face. He dropped to the ground and Le Ray stole his coat and wallet. Despite the seriousness of his situation Le Ray felt sympathy for the poor man he attacked, a 'brutal act of violence against an innocent civilian' as he would describe it, but he justified his actions as self-defence under the conditions of war. If Le Ray had been caught with a German civilian's identity papers and wallet, as an escaped prisoner of war he would have been shot on the spot.

The stolen money bought several train tickets which carried Le Ray closer to the Swiss border, at Stuttgart he bought another ticket to move him close to the border with a plan to scale the Alps to neutral territory. After nearly a week on the run and with limited food he decided he had not the strength for such a climb. Still using the stolen identity papers Le Ray bought a ticket to Singen where he knew the border was less mountainous and would provide easy crossing. Eventually at evening *Appel* the Wehrmacht guards at Colditz realized they were missing a prisoner and set about searching the Castle, finding no clue as to where Le Ray was or how he had escaped. Le Ray had now arrived at Singen, near the Swiss border, before deciding to walk the last few miles toward Switzerland. As he moved through a forest toward the Swiss border he heard shouting and guard dogs. Quickly he backed away, climbing a large tree where he hid until dark when the danger had passed. Fearing the guards would now be on high alert, he abandoned his plan and returned to the train station at Gottmandingen, it was the last station before the border with Switzerland. Le Ray had run out of money and did not possess the right papers to cross the border, he hid in buses at the end of the platform to ponder his next move. At 11:30 pm the train from Singen pulled in and ground to a halt as the few passengers crossed paths through the train doors. Calm was restored to the station and the station master blew his whistle and turned to move toward the warmth of the ticket office. Le Ray seized his only chance. Jumping from the bushes onto the platform he lowered himself to the ground next to the tracks as the train slowly moved forwards. The train headlights gave him enough light to climb up the front of the train and sit between the two bumpers, Le Ray held on for dear life, wondering if his actions were madness but as the train gathered speed he relaxed and enjoyed moving through the cool air of the spring night. Fortunately, he was still dressed in the dark coat he had stolen and sat upright between the bumpers and allowed his feet to dangle inches above the rails as they flashed by, until in the distance he saw the enemy guard post. Curling up his legs he was invisible as the glare of the headlamps made it impossible for guards to spot him. The Frenchman felt a wild surge of hope and pride as he zoomed under the bridge and into Switzerland. Alain Le Ray had succeeded in leaving Colditz, the escape-proof prison, in just 46 days.

The French Embassy welcomed Le Ray with open arms, and he described his escape in great detail to the French Consul who proudly informed the British Embassy in Switzerland. Eventually word reached Colditz and wild celebrations were enjoyed. A French officer had not only absconded from the escape-proof castle but escaped to Switzerland in only seven weeks: the surge in hope for the prisoners of war was enormous. Le Ray survived the war and was promoted to Lieutenant Colonel, serving in Indo-China in 1953 and Algeria during the uprising against French rule. In the late 1960s he commanded the 27th Infantry Division of the French Army and was promoted again to General de Corps D'Armee. In 1976 he published a book on his escape entitled *Première à Colditz* ('First in Colditz') and held the Croix de Guerre and the Grand Cross of the Legion d'Honneur. During retirement Le Ray enjoyed skiing, even into his nineties.

Lieutenant Boucheron – France

Feigning medical illness was one way to escape the confines of Colditz Castle, but if a prisoner of war managed to convince the guards and medical staff of the Wehrmacht that a visit to hospital or the dentist was required, it was always under armed guard. In addition, any stay in a civilian or military hospital was short. The Germans thought nothing of marching a prisoner back to a train station on the return journey to Colditz the day after a major operation. The difficulty of a hospital escape was such that up to this point only one man had successfully made a 'home run' by feigning illness and then absconding from a medical facility, the Pole Lieutenant Kroner.

In March 1941 two French officers made an attempt to escape using a Polish method which had proved successful, descending into a small garden from the canteen windows. Sadly, Jacques Charvet and Andre Boucheron made too much noise removing the iron bars across the window and they alerted the guard who promptly came to investigate. Fortunately, Charvet and Boucheron managed to avoid detection and slipped back into the French quarters. Unfortunately, the guards deduced that the culprits must be British or Polish, as their quarters were closest to the canteen. They summarily dragged every British and Polish prisoner from their beds to stand on parade in freezing temperatures whilst Charvet and Boucheron slept soundly. Needless to say, after his actions proved to create international diplomatic tensions, Boucheron redoubled his efforts to escape.

Some months later Boucheron became unwell with an inflamed appendix. However, the last two patients to visit the hospital had escaped under armed guard, and the furore that followed was still evident. Lieutenants Just and Bednarski had been recaptured but not until the latter had reached Krakow and returned to Colditz with a considerable amount of valuable information that other prisoners could utilize. The Tierarzt (veterinarian) sent Boucheron to hospital at Zeitz after a thorough physical examination, but there was no doubt about his condition. Whilst at hospital Boucheron decided to grasp his chance despite his condition, on 25 September he broke into the hospital storeroom, exchanged his clothes for civilian ones and calmly walked out of the hospital. After over a week on the run Boucheron was captured by police at Bonn, with his appendix still intact, and placed in a Stalag near Arnoldsweiler. As the guards from Colditz were dispatched to collect him they arrived to be informed that Boucheron had absconded yet again after convincing the camp doctor that his condition was life-threatening and he had been taken to a hospital at Munster-Eifel. Boucheron performed the same course of action; after a swift change of clothes he absconded and arrived safely in France. Upon returning empty-handed to the Castle, the Tierarzt commented that Boucheron's appendix would have made interesting medical history. There is no record of Boucheron having an operation on his appendix whilst in France!

Lieutenant Guy de Frondeville – France

Guy-Jean-Michel Lambert de Frondeville was born on 12 March 1917 in Evreux. The son of the Marquis de Frondeville, he completed his studies at the Institution Sainte-Marie-de-Monceau and at the Collège Stanislas in Paris and later enrolled at the École Polytechnique in 1938. When war broke out in 1939 de Frondeville was captured during fierce fighting in the battle for France and became a prisoner of war at Offlag VI-D, Lieutenant de Frondeville escaped soon after arriving at the camp but was recaptured and despatched to IV-C Colditz. In the many hours of incarceration de Frondeville worked on his false identity and travel documents, by the Christmas of 1941 the forgeries were of a very good standard.

The German guards were in high spirits in mid-December 1941. Leave postings had given the officers time with their families over Christmas and a plot to spring Lieutenant Baron von Lynden and Captain Steenhouwer from the Castle had been foiled. On 16 December two 'German' officers presented themselves at the gatehouse and the guard saluted and unlocked the door, and the two officers made their way down the path toward the town. The guard realized he had forgotten to ask to see their passes. Running after them he shouted for the officers to wait. Ahey replied in good German that it was all right as they would be right back. Still suspicious, the guard was called out and Dutch officers von Lynden and Steenhouwer were confined to solitary. The following day French Lieutenants Prot, Durand-Hornus and de Frondeville were in a party of seven, five POWs and two guards, who required the services of the town dentist. On a foggy afternoon the men drifted out of the dentist and three of the five men darted off, all in different directions. The guards were at a loss what to do, they dare not fire their weapons and could not give chase as two of the men had not moved. There was no alternative but to march the two prisoners back to the Castle and raise the alarm.

Prot and de Frondeville were reunited on the road to Leipzig but separated for safety. Travelling by train de Frondeville made excellent progress and once into French territory he enjoyed some home comforts from his country men who ensured he was cared for along the route to Vichy France. Once there, de Frondville wrote a postcard to inform his Senior Officer of his successful escape. Under the Vichy government France agreed an armistice with Hitler, the latter wishing to focus on Britain and North Africa, so de Frondeville could not actively continue the fight against the Nazis. The French forces were reduced to an armistice army of 100,000 men (Hitler selected the number as it matched the Treaty of Versailles restrictions placed on the German armed forces in 1919) and the 1.2 million prisoners of war remained in captivity. De Frondeville enrolled at the École des Mines de Paris as a student engineer, which sent him for internships in Tunisia, Algeria and Morocco. Returning to France in October 1942, he was sent to take courses at the École des Mines in Saint-Etienne and shortly after this posting de Frondeville was assigned as a mining engineer to Saint-Etienne. During this period, he was rarely at his post. De Frondeville continued the fight against Hitler in the Resistance from 1 October 1943 to 26 August 1944. For the remainder of the war he was an active member of the FFC resistance (Vlite Thermopyles network, where he was Lyon regional leader) until 9 May 1945. De Frondeville was promoted to artillery reserve captain on 1 June 1945.

Guy de Frondeville survived the war and embarked on an extensive career, finding time to marry Jacqueline de Malleray and raise eight children. Initially he worked for the Mines Corps to the General Commission for German and Austrian Affairs. Latterly he was promoted to become head of the Mines Service in Saarland, and deputy to the Director of Industrial Production for the French zone of occupation in Germany. On 1 January 1949, he was appointed to the Interministerial Committee for European Economic Cooperation Questions, which reported directly to the Presidency of the Council. He was placed at the disposal of the Directorate of External Economic Relations (DREE) until 1951, in charge of work relating to the Marshall Plan and Permanent Secretary of the Supply Commission. In the same year de Frondeville was seconded as chief engineer Deputy to the Director of Public Works of Tunisia. During his stay in Tunisia, he practiced diving and underwater archaeology leading an excavation in 1953–4 on the Mahdia ship wreck. In 1956 he published the book *Visitors to the Sea*.

An Officer of the Legion of Honor, de Frondeville was amongst the eldest surviving members of those prisoners incarcerated in Oflag IV-C, passing away on 29 April 2008.

Lieutenant Pierre Mairesse Lebrun – France

Of the nationalities incarcerated in Colditz Castle, the French produced escape plans of cunning flair and Gallic ingenuity, so much so that the more stoic nations examined such schemes with a mixture or incredulity and downright mirth. Pierre Mairesse Lebrun's escape was remarkable for its daring, the cavalry lieutenant had escaped twice before and had been recaptured close to the Swiss border. Naturally Lebrun attempted to leave Colditz and on June 9 1941 the Castle received a call from Grossbothen police station asking if they were missing a prisoner. A man dressed in the smartest civilian clothes (far too smart for wartime Germans), beautifully polished shoes and a monocle had attempted to buy a train ticket to Leipzig with out of date money. To Lebrun's shock the note had Kaiser Wilhelm II on it and was no longer legal tender in Nazi Germany, Lebrun was later recaptured and, after twenty-one days solitary began plotting a new bid for freedom.

As a frequent escaper and a Lieutenant, Lebrun was afforded a cell in the Castle, which meant his exercise period was from 12:30 pm to 2:30 pm and was guarded by an NCO (Feldwebel) and three armed guards. For a number of weeks Lebrun would dash 800 yards, gradually improving his speed and stamina. In addition he gathered supplies from his comrades including a silk cravat into which he stuffed a razor, soap, a little sugar and some chocolate. In the days preceding his bid for freedom fellow prisoners smuggled extra rations to his cell, as well as 30 Reichsmarks obtained from a friendly guard. Lebrun was ready to go dressed in running shorts, a short-sleeved shirt, a leather sleeveless jacket, gloves and plimsoles. Five exercise periods passed with none providing the conditions for escape. Guards were positioned in unfavourable spots for an attempt which would have bordered on suicide. Finally, on 2 July the sky was overcast, the guards were distracted and with his comrade Odry the pair circled the exercise field for an hour before marking the spot with a small stone, where Lebrun would jump the 8ft-high wired fence. If Lebrun made the jump, with Odry's arm providing extra momentum, he would be faced with a 100-yard dash and a brick wall to scale. Odry was informed this would be the last circuit of the field, with guards busy chatting with prisoners. Odry positioned himself next to the stone with hands clasped. Lebrun ran toward him and was heaved into the air clearing the barbed wire fence and landing on the opposite side. Immediately he was on his feet desperately running in a zigzag toward the wall. A sentry raised the alarm after encouraging shouts from prisoners and three shots were fired. As Lebrun reached the wall, he knew he had to scale it quickly whilst they reloaded. As he successfully landed on a path the other side of the wall he made for a wood as the siren signalling an escaped POW blared across the valley. Fortunately, the officer did not scale the wall himself in pursuit, preferring to report the escape in the guardroom and alert a search party, made up of police, sniffer dogs and the Hitler Youth.

Lebrun lay flat on his stomach moving slowly backwards and raising flattened corn storks as he made his way toward the centre of the field unseen by farm workers. When night fell he waited until 10:30 pm before rising and following the River Mulde, partially to throw the dogs off his scent and in order to reach Zwickau. For two days and three nights it rained continuously. As Lebrun was dressed in light clothing and shorts this made him look suspicious, so he travelled at night and slept rough in woods or cornfields. On 5 July the sun began to shine and Lebrun walked into Zwickau with dry clothes on his back. He stole a bicycle so that as he could pass for a German tourist cycling his way through the countryside. Lebrun now made for the Swiss border which was nearly 400 miles away. The bicycle was a perfect means of transport as he did not have to converse with fellow passengers on a train or bus. After eight days of cycling, stealing food and sleeping rough, the Swiss border was within reach. However, disaster struck as the bicycle collapsed in a heap beyond repair, Lebrun did not want to attract attention, so quickly stowed the remains in a hedge and took the pump with him, the only salvageable part. Continuing on foot Lebrun could see the border. He fought the urge to burst into a run as a patrolling local policeman made a beeline for him. Waiting until the man was close enough Lebrun launched himself at the man beating him with the bicycle pump before sprinting for the woodland border and freedom.

Lebrun had made the third French 'home run'. The Colditz guards had entered his cell to find a neatly packed suitcase with a note and some strong German sausage next to it, to throw the guard dogs off his scent. The note read: 'If I succeed, I would be grateful if you would arrange for my personal possessions to be sent to the following address …May God help me!' After a few months the suitcase full of Colditz mementoes arrived in Marseilles. Lebrun was grateful for it, describing the guards as 'true soldiers'.

Lieutenant Jacques Prot – France

Dentistry became a bugbear for Kommandant Schmidt and his staff as the Castle could only provide the most basic of fillings for the prisoners in Colditz. With skilled medical professionals in short supply in civilian Germany, the Castle had to make do with a veterinarian as the medical officer for some months. The new medical officer was quickly inundated with appointments from prisoners of war keen to exploit his naivete, claiming every medical condition under the sun. Any dental work beyond the simple fillings on offer had to be done at the town dentist.

On 17 December 1941 the guards were having a Christmas meal led by Egger's deputy, Oberstleutnant von Kirchbach who had lost an arm in the First World War and was far from a stickler for discipline. The party was disturbed when the guard NCO burst in and told von Kirchbach that three French officers had scarpered from the town dentists, Lieutenant Prot, Durand-Hornus and de Frondeville. Operation Mousetrap was initiated and seven guards were sent to the dentist in the town to organize the search. It transpired that in the early evening fog and mist three French lieutenants had taken the opportunity to flee when leaving the dentists surgery. The guard with them could not run after all three as they had split up, and he could not fire his weapon blindly into the fog for fear of endangering civilians. Jacques Prot had noticed the weather from the window upstairs and made up his mind to run once they were on the street, he even took the hat and coat belonging to the dentist for civilian clothes. Despite carrying with false papers in case an opportunity to escape arose, Prot's chances were not high as fewer trains were running in the evening. He made his way to Leipzig on foot, rejoining his friend de Frondeville enroute. At Leipzig the two men separated for safety and Prot boarded a train the following day which gave him safe passage through Cologne toward Aachen.

As Prot neared the border with France he suddenly realized that civilians either side of him were clutching an additional paper to move through the frontier, one he did not possess. The forged papers from Colditz were out of date. In front of him he saw the border was heavily guarded and as the travellers shuffled forward he was just a few feet from the guard who would demand his papers. In a moment of escape flair Prot seized the suitcase of the astonished man standing next to him and bolted through the check-in desk and set off at a terrific pace. Naturally the man who lost his case caused an almighty scene, demanding the German guards pursue Prot with haste, but as soon as the guards had understood what had happened they called of the chase, believing it to be the simple matter of a theft of luggage. It was a brilliant and inspired move by Prot. Nine days after leaving the dentist Prot surprised his family in Paris by appearing on their doorstep on Christmas Eve. Whilst in Paris he arranged for the return of the suitcase to the enraged Belgian traveller with apologies and a full explanation of what had happened (Prot found the Belgian traveller's name and address inside the suitcase). A letter of apology and some fine French coffee was posted to the town dentist for the loss of his hat and coat.

In 1942 Prot travelled into the Free French zone and boarded a ship which docked in Tunis. Joining the Algerian 67th Artillery Regiment, Lieutenant Prot fought bravely in the Tunisian campaign and reached Casino in early 1944. The French Algerian battalions focussed their assault on the right flank under the command of General Julius Ringel with the objective of capturing Mont Belveder to help cut off Monte Cassino from the rear. In the first offensive on 29 January 1944 Prot gave his life for France.

Lieutenant Theodore Tattischeff

France

Vladimir Lenin headed opposition to Tsar Nicholas II in the early twentieth century leading to the Bolshevik Revolution in 1917. Russia descended into a bloody civil war with the White forces, consisting of Conservative elites and army officers, battling against the red wall of Bolshevism. Lieutenant Tattischeff was a Frenchman of White Russian origin swept up by the

Germans in the Battle for France, and as a persistent escaper he was sent to Colditz.

The Nazi High Command were keen to use the prisoners of war in captivity as slave labour or future hostages. Colditz housed a number of *Prominentes*, including Giles Romilly, the nephew of Winston Churchill. The camp Kommandant Colonel Schmidt was requested to take a lenient approach to the White Russian contingent and this extended to the festivities of the Russian Orthodox faith. The hope was that Hitler could use their dislike and battle experience in cold conditions against Stalin's Red Army. Colonel Schmidt permitted the White Russian contingent more freedom including moving the prisoners to the town *Schützenhaus*, a camp in the town where workers were housed, mostly of Russian origin. Dressed in tattered green uniforms their emaciated appearance shocked the officers inside Colditz. The *Schützenhaus* was also under Schmidt's authority and was more relaxed than the Oflag. So much so, that when the festivities in the Russian Orthodox calendar approached Eggers helped to organize a visit to Colditz from the Orthodox Bishop of Dresden and the choir of the Church of St Simeon Stylites on the evening of 17 July 1941. The prisoners from the town *Schützenhaus* were escorted under armed guard to the main castle and filed into the chapel to hear the choir and enjoy the service. After the performance the prisoners mingled with the members of the choir and Tattischeff was seen chatting with a Miss Hoffman. With male attention limited due to so many men away fighting in the war, Miss Hoffman was so taken with Tattischeff she helped him leave the Castle with the choir and the Bishop. Once out of the Castle the pair made the short trip to Leisnig together and returned to Miss Hoffman's house in Dresden.

At evening *Appel* in the *Schützenhaus* one prisoner was missing. Naturally it was assumed that Tattischeff was still in Colditz and the Castle was alerted. Evening *Appel* at the Castle did not unearth Tattischeff but word had spread that he may have escaped with the choir and the other prisoners from the *Schützenhaus*. The other prisoners in the Castle were suitably impressed that he had managed such a daring escape but also that he had manage to charm a young lady in such a short time. Tattischeff spent the next few days with Miss Hoffman before travelling to Lyon and freedom, but Ms Hoffman was tracked down, arrested and sent to a labour camp.

A final note on Colonel Schmidt. The Kommandant and Eggers were not inclined to prohibit further instances of goodwill to the men of Colditz. Both men were always viewed as fair and considerate, far from the dyed-in-the-wool Nazis many would expect from the Kommandant of the highest security prisoner of war camp in Germany and a senior officer. On 15 April 1945 Colditz was liberated by American GIs and Eggers, as Security Officer, ensured that all 1,400 items of property belonging to the prisoners were returned before the peaceful fall of the Castle. Eggers was the only English-speaking officer and worked with the American troops to ensure a calm transfer of power, in peacetime Eggers would suffer great hardship with his decision to remain in what would become Soviet-controlled East Germany. The land he and his wife owned was in East Germany, as well as his former post as a school master, and he did not make efforts to cross into the West. In 1946 he was arrested by the feared NKVD, the Soviet secret police, and interrogated. Eggers wrongly assumed he was in no danger as a former First World War veteran who had no connections to the Nazi Party. The NKVD searched for informers within the Castle placed there by the Gestapo or for any potential connection with the West through his prisoners. Eggers was portrayed as an enemy of the state by the NKVD and sentenced to ten years hard labour for aiding the Fascist regime. Over 10,000 prisoners were housed at Special NVKD camp number 1 and conditions were horrendous, beatings and starvation being commonplace. It was only in 1955 as part of Khruschev's de-Stalinization that improved relations with the West that Eggers was finally released, weighing just 110lbs. Eggers settled in Lake Constance, not far from Singen, the route used by so many Colditz officers who escaped, where he wrote his memoirs of Colditz. Eggers passed away in 1974 at the age of 84. Colonel Schmidt retired on 31 July 1942 when he was 70 years old and moved from Dresden to Klein Wanzleben. Schmidt was arrested by the GPU (the secret police) and interned in the camps at Klein Wanzleben and Reval. He passed away in a hospital in Riga in 1947 as a result of the harsh conditions in the camps.

Lieutenant Élisée Alban Darthenay – France

Lieutenant Fahy was wounded in an unsavoury incident by Hauptmann Muller in June 1942 and required hospital treatment. It was from his sickbed at Hohnstein-Erstthal that he absconded, much to Muller's embarrassment. A few days later Fahy was recaptured at Kaufungen and returned to Colditz. Three weeks later Lieutenant Elisee-Alban Darthenay was due to visit the same hospital and Fahy gave him a detailed account of the areas with weak security.

Élisée Alban Darthenay was born on 3rd January 1913 in Montrouge and enrolled with the French infantry as a Second Lieutenant in 1937. During the Battle for France, Darthenay was stationed on the Maginot Line near Alsace and, as the German advance pushed the French infantry back, he was defending bridges across the Saone River when he was captured. Held in camps between June 1941 and early 1942 he was deemed sufficiently dangerous to be transferred to Colditz in July of that year. Darthenay realized that he had a much better chance of a successful escape if he were already outside the Castle walls, and hospitalization was the best opportunity. At the request of Reinhold Eggers, the town dentist was now coming into the Castle to perform surgeries.

A few weeks prior to his attempt, Darthenay received a parcel from his wife of some light civilian clothes which could be worn under his uniform. Provided with excellent papers, he gained all the necessary details from Fahy and allowed the 'symptoms' to develop which fooled the German medics. Once at Hohnstein-Erstthal Darthenay made a home run and found his family before promptly joining the Resistance of Ain and Haut-Jura in November 1943 where he was given a new identity; Jean-Louis Naucourt. For five months Darthenay worked to disrupt German supply lines and sabotage railway lines, gaining the nickname 'the Mute' as he did not speak about his activities to anyone. On Good Friday he was arrested with four other men and suspected of being involved in Resistance activities in the Haut-Jura area, they were imprisoned at the school in Oyannax. After four days of horrendous torture and interrogation 'the Mute' had revealed nothing and the party were led to a small village named Sieges in the Jura on 11 April.

The German troops held an identity parade as each member of the village filed past the men, but not one of the villagers gave them away. Furious the Germans set the village on fire, rounded up all the men in the district, some women and children too, and sent them to a camp in Germany. The five men of the Resistance, including Darthenay, were lined up against a farm wall and machine-gunned to death.

Lieutenant Elisee-Alban Darthenay was posthumously awarded the Knight of the Legion of Honour on 26 April 26 1945 and the Croix de Guerre for his bravery.

Lieutenant Navelet and Lieutenant Odry – France

Lieutenant Odry was the Frenchman involved in helping Pierre Mairesse Lebrun pull off his daring 'leapfrog' escape from the exercise park in 1941. A committed escaper and popular member of the Colditz camp, Odry had a reputation amongst the guards as a man not to be trusted and persistently on the lookout for escape or plotting to escape. The 'cupped hands assist' to Lebrun had solidified his reputation.

An opportunity for Odry and three other French Lieutenants in Colditz arrived in October 1941 as a bout of cold weather and ill health combined to send many prisoners to the German vet (there was no doctor available at the time). Pierre Odry had persistent abdominal pain with a possible grumbling appendix or appendicitis. Lieutenant Navelet was suffering from continued painful swelling and fluid on his knee, whilst Jacques Charvet and Levy were unlikely to have been ill, but no doubt saw an opportunity to be liberated from the Castle. They had worked with Colditz POW French doctor Captain M Le Guet who had convinced the camp vet that hospital investigation was required. Considering Odry's record of three escape attempts prior to Colditz and his key involvement in numerous escapes, the Germans would never have agreed to a hospital trip without very convincing evidence. Nevertheless, Odry, Navelet and the others were permitted to visit the hospital that was attached to camp Oflag IV-D at Elsterhorst which housed French officers. It was a significant distance to travel for the genuinely sick. The trip from Colditz involved two train journeys and a three to four kilometre walk from the station on roads running through countryside. The administration formalities at Colditz before release from the Castle added further time to the journey which would take almost a complete day to reach Elsterhorst.

Despite the condition of Navelet and Odry (Odry had had an appendectomy and Navelet's knee had not significantly improved), the men were considering the opportunity for escape. The four Frenchmen soon discovered the inevitable when they arrived at the hospital, it was well guarded. What the men needed now was time to recover before making their move. They did not get it. Despite Odry being very weak from his operation, the German authorities decided all four were to return to Colditz Castle on 14 October. Charvet and Levy were fit and able to escape, they had noticed that the Elsterhorst road back towards the railway station crossed open ground and scrubby heathland with scattered pines. More dense vegetation came with a rise in the ground and the road pushed on through a wood with oak and beech trees. The heart of the wood was the best point to make a getaway. Armed with excellent forged papers and being acutely aware of the border crossings into France, the men decided that it was worth the risk.

Upon receiving medical treatment the POW's were woken at 4.00 am and were to be fully dressed and ready with their luggage for a full search at 4.30 am. At 5.00 am they departed from the hospital on foot with their armed escort to cover the two or so miles to the railway station. The train would depart around 6.00 am. The early start was in Navelet and Odry's favour as it was not light at that time of the year until at least 7.00 am, so the journey to the station would be in darkness. It was a cold morning and next to the hospital bedroom, a stove was burning in the head nurse's office. Levy managed to give some hot coffee to the POWs whilst they were searched along with their luggage. The escort guards, consisting of one sergeant and a soldier warmed themselves by the stove, while two French POW soldiers from the camp party waited outside with a handcart they would use to carry luggage up to the station. The guards welcomed the hot drinks Levy gave them and the freezing sentry at the gate was invited under the porch of the open door for a cup. Whilst he was there, Navelet, Charvet and Levy went outside to put their luggage on the handcart. Odry could carry nothing and was too weak from his operation to attempt an escape, but he would do everything possible to give the others a chance.

Once the official paperwork and formalities were completed the party set off towards the station. Navelet had decided that with his lack of mobility his chances of getting away were far less than those of Charvet and Levy. Once he gave the prearranged signal, each prisoner would run away into the darkness in separate directions, shedding their military coats at the first opportunity. Odry did not expect to get far but he was determined to be a nuisance and help confuse the guards as much as possible. The party trailed slowly into the woods, the two Frenchmen from the camp pulling the cart and Navelet, Charvet, Levy and Odry being flanked by the two guards. In the darkest part of the woods, Navelet gave the signal and the three men ran off into the trees leaving Odry behind, who made a vain attempt to shuffle away before being dragged back. The escort sergeant was taken by surprise and took time to get his pistol out and fire several shots. The men had already disappeared into the undergrowth.

Furious with how easily the prisoners had escaped, the escort sergeant marched the party back to the hospital at Elsterhorst with Odry, this decision giving the missing men vital minutes. Navelet, who was the least mobile of the three, worked his way back to the road and hobbled to the station where he caught the train without being stopped. The search party was still being organized back at the hospital as his train pulled out of the station. Lieutenant Charvet reached Kassel where it is believed he boarded a train to Aachen but caught the wrong connection and ended up travelling in the wrong direction towards Dusseldorf. By a total coincidence he met up with Levy and they journeyed back to Aachen, spending the night in a nearby wood. Thinking quickly, they stated they were just French rankers and were sent to an ordinary camp at Arnoldsweiler. After three weeks of doing a sterling job of wasting the time of the German guards by concocting differing stories of their true identity they had eventually let it be known they were from Oshatz in East Germany – another fabrication. Whilst travelling on a train headed for East Germany Charvet escaped again, breaking out of the train and jumping for freedom. With no false papers, money or food, he was recaptured at Helmstett, exhausted, Charvet confessed he was from Oflag-4C and was returned to Colditz where Levy greeted him.

Odry was roughly dragged back to the hospital and left to rest whist the guard raised the alarm and organized a swift search of the woodland. It was in this confusion that Odry simply walked off to the local bus stop nearby appearing as a normal patient. Odry would eventually pass through to the Free French sector via train. Navelet made a successful home run back to France where he went into hiding.

Lieutenant Rene Collin – France

Under the terms of the Geneva Convention the Kommandant was required to give his prisoners fresh air and exercise. Initially, the main courtyard within the Castle was an open-air space of some 35 by 45 yards and provided suitable room for walking and somewhere to escape the quarters with barred windows and stuffy air. Beyond the Castle there was an exercise field which Kommandant Schmidt permitted the prisoners to use despite the obvious challenges this posed for his guards who preferred to retain the prisoners in the Castle with hall walls and secure windows. However, the exercise field offered the opportunity for organized sports which would keep the officers occupied and wean them away from thoughts of escape. Guards also took the opportunity of empty rooms to conduct unofficial searches to find contraband or escape equipment. When Alain Le Ray became the first man to escape Colditz Castle and the German guards were at a loss to explain how he managed to do what seemed impossible, their thoughts turned toward the exercise park. Schmidt promptly ended daily exercise in the park and the prisoners complained. The British contingent filed two complaints of contraventions of the Geneva Convention: the first was about the loss of daily exercise in the park and the second that no prisoners should be collectively punished for the actions of another. The matter was referred to the Swiss Government as the neutral power, and they discussed the matter with Kommandant Schmidt, who relented and reinstated the exercise in the park.

Security around the exercise was extremely tight. The minimum number of prisoners was thirty. If fewer appeared for exercise the trip to the park was cancelled, but if an escape was on sometimes too many prisoners appeared but each time the men went down to the field it was a raucous affair. The guards requested five ranks, which was lost in translation as prisoners made it impossible to perform a proper count with shouting and jostling ruining the proposed ranks. Men would jump into the rank just after the count, or walk back inside at the last minute to fudge the numbers. Lieutenant Rene Collin observed all of this and realized that following his compatriot Le Ray offered the best possibility of escape. However, where the path turned and offered Le Ray the opportunity to climb the bank and enter Terrace House, the Germans had closed this avenue of escape. The column was now flanked by guards with further guards at the end with dogs. In addition, the pace of march was now much quicker, especially with a dog behind the prisoners. They were forced into a quick march through the two gateways and into the paddock. But Collin had spotted that there was a summer house in one corner with open sides, a relic from the days Colditz was a hospital. This was the chance he had been looking for. The summer house had rafters and a pointed roof which held the structure in place. Collin decided he would hide in the rafters of the summer house and hope the chaos of the counting by guards would hide one missing prisoner. For the next few days Collin managed to gather some German money and rations alongside some clothes that would pass for a civilian as well as a small bag. Collin had decided he would pose as a doctor travelling to see a patient. This would allow him to buy short journey railway tickets and make his way to Vichy France slowly but safely. Then Collin had some good fortune at the expense of other prisoners' escapes. The canteen tunnel inspired by Pat Reid was exposed along with ten British and two Polish officers including the Senior British Officer at the time, Colonel German. Reinhold Eggers was delighted, having confiscated 85 Marks, 150lbs of supplies and numerous forged papers. The Germans very pleased, but they dropped their guard.

On 31 May 1941 Collin lined up with the other prisoners and the parade to the field was its usual boisterous affair, men jostled with each other, shouting across lines, 'accidentally' bumping into the guards and prisoners joining the ranks at the last moment to be replaced by three or four men. Collin had help as Pierre Mairesse Lebrun was orchestrating the chaos from the French side as the men were marched down toward the exercise field. Once they arrived the usual diversions were acted out, football matches and arguments broke out between French officers which distracted the guards, Collin slipped up into the rafters unseen. At the end of the allotted time the guards blew whistles and the men slowly fell into ranks with the usual barrack-room behaviour and were led through the gate up toward the Castle. At this moment Collin had an urge to climb down from the rafters and cut through the wire with his homemade cutters and run for it, but he displayed true escapers' calmness and sat still, waiting for night to fall.

As soon as the Castle was in darkness, the paddock remained quiet and still. The guards had not realized they were a man short. There would be evening *Appel* but the prisoners were organized enough to cover the absence of one man so early in the war. The guards were still under the impression that Colditz was escape proof and they were yet to grow wise to the cunning of the prisoners. Collin lowered himself to the ground and crept toward the wire fence, cutting through to the other side he replaced the wires as best he could so it did not appear an obvious escape route and made his way to the nearest town to board a train. By purchasing tickets for shorter routes Collin avoided suspicion. He travelled swiftly toward Vichy France explaining to fellow passengers he was making a short trip to visit a patient. Rene Collin was the second home run.

The Indian Escape

Captain Birendra Nath Mazumdar – India

The son of a distinguished surgeon from the city of Gaya in north-east India, Mazumdar was born into a high-caste Hindu family with close ties to the British Raj, under which the family had flourished. Mazumdar's father was acclimatized to the English way of life and many of his patients came from the military ranks of the East India Company and Mazumdar was educated at the finest elite schools in the country, modelled on the English educational system. Despite this Mazumdar grew up to despise the empire and the Raj, witnessing its brutality and the superiority of the British. Caught between his nationalist feelings and the anglicized upbringing instilled by his father, Mazumdar continued to live by Victorian standards; fair play, integrity and duty. In 1931 he left India as a skilled doctor fluent in English, German, French, Urdu, Hindi and Bengali; his aim was to become a member of the Royal College of Surgeons. Held in the highest regard by his fellow countrymen, upon arriving in London he was viewed as just another Indian by his newly adopted nation. Mazumdar remained in the capital for many years until war broke out and he volunteered for the Royal Army Medical Corps. He was given the rank of Captain and swore an oath to King George VI and despatched to the 17th Base Hospital in Étaples in France to work as a general medical officer. He was the only non-white member of the British Army at this point in the war.

In May 1940, with the Nazi war machine closing in on victory in the Battle for France Mazumdar bravely led a convoy of ambulances with 500 wounded Allied servicemen toward the city of Boulogne-sur-mer to join the evacuation to the United Kingdom. As the convoy travelled north it passed through a village named Neufchatel-en-Bray and met resistance. German tanks blocked the road as Mazumdar's convoy approached. They were 85 miles from Boulogne. Without warning the Panzers opened fire, destroying two of the ambulances. Mazumdar helped pull survivors from the wreckage and treated their wounds. The convoy remained still whilst the Panzer tanks waited for their next move, Mazumdar raised a white handkerchief and approached the lead tank. In perfect English the German commander gave his apologies for opening fire and took the entire party prisoners of war. Marched over 100 miles, many of the wounded struggled, eventually the party was loaded onto filthy coal barges and slowly progressed down the canal system toward Germany. Conditions were horrendous with human excrement underfoot and disease rife. Mazumdar protested and this began his journey of frustration and anger with his German captives. Matters became worse when at last the barges had reached Germany, the men were taken on a two-day march to a prison in Kassel. Each man was searched and had all their belongings taken. Mazumdar was deprived of his silver cigarette lighter and case and instructed to have his head shaved. Mazumdar protested vigorously, citing the Hindu faith reserved the right to shave the head of the son if one of his parents had passed away. After a vociferous argument he was forcibly taken away to the cells and suffered the ignominy of a head shaving. Relations between Mazumdar and his captors deteriorated further and at an alarming rate when he protested about conditions for his patients. He provided the Germans with a list of required improvements such as improved medical supplies, warm clothing for winter, fresh fruit and vegetables for the sick and improvements in hygiene to halt the spread of tuberculosis in the prison. Mazumdar was moved to another prison, and then another, going through twelve in all. In each camp he exposed the Germans for failing to keep to the Geneva Convention including expressing concern at the appalling bread rations which were mouldy and insufficient for 1,500 men in transit to a prisoner of war camp. Throughout the camps Mazumdar worked in he was regarded with the highest esteem as a medic, working diligently and acting as a credit to his commission. With his high regard for English soldiers and excellent care for the wounded, Mazumdar should have been celebrated, yet he faced discrimination from his patients and isolation. When Red Cross parcels arrived, the men would not provide him with one, nor share their rations. Mazumdar was viewed with suspicion from both sides. Fellow officers in the British Army gave him the nickname 'Jumbo' after a famous elephant in London Zoo. He detested the name.

At many points during his captivity Mazumdar was asked to join the Axis powers. According to Nazi ideology and the principle of the Aryan Race all non-whites were subhuman, but those who belonged to nations seeking independence from the British could be of considerable value. At Kassel camp he was interviewed by a young Indian man and the Gestapo who offered him the opportunity to switch sides and make radio broadcasts asking other Indian nationals to fight the British and end the Raj. Mazumdar refused. The young Indian then asked Mazumdar to broadcast to a German audience only. The reply was the same and he was frogmarched back to his cell. In 1941 the Germans tried again at Marienberg camp where Mazumdar was asked to travel to Berlin and make a radio broadcast. When he refused a revolver was pushed into his back and he feared the worst. Without warning he was forced out of the room and bundled onto a train for Berlin. Taken from the train station in central Berlin, Mazumdar was brought to an office block where two German officers were awaiting his arrival. The questions remained the same. Will you broadcast? Why do you serve the British Army when the British deny your country independence? Each time Mazumdar refused to co-operate citing his commission and oath to King George VI. Unperturbed the more senior officer offered him female company. At this Mazumdar exploded with rage, shouting back 'If you think my honour can be bought with a woman, you are very wrong'. In autumn 1942 his file was labelled as being *Deutschfeindlich*, anti-German, and he was dispatched to Oflag IVC Colditz.

The mistrust of men held in captivity upon greeting a new inmate was high, and with good reason. Men suspected Mazumdar of being a spy for India, or possibly Germany. In time, he won over each prisoner of war in Colditz and became known as 'Jumbo' as he diligently cared for British officers with two events underlining his integrity. The first came after Pat Reid had been sent some Upmann Havana cigars encased in aluminium tubes by the '13 Club', a group of university friends from King's College who heard he was incarcerated in Colditz and sent him some light relief. The cargo was three months in transit but arrived safely at Colditz in April 1943. This event coincided with the start of the 'escape season' with the German

Guards launching their counter offensive and carrying out searches of the British quarters. This was followed by an officer 'personal search' which was often much more invasive. Books, papers, cupboards, tables, chairs and stools upturned or emptied, floorboards ripped up and beds left tipped over, the quarters resembled a dishevelled pigsty. The British posted a placard on the main door which read; 'You are invited to visit an example of Nazi culture'.

Mazumdar was called to this scene when Lieutenant Monty Bissell refused to undress unless in the presence of a doctor or a priest. The Germans, perplexed but respectful of his wishes, summoned the doctor and Mazumdar at once realized what was afoot. Bissell had smoked one of Pat Reid's Upmann Havana cigars and put the aluminium case to excellent use as something the men of Colditz described as an 'arse-creeper'. Bissell had found an ingenious method of hiding German money, a map and other personal effects which would be ideal for a planned escape and was keen that the German guards did not confiscate it. Using considerable discretion, the Indian doctor ensured the item remained undiscovered and quickly made friends in the British camp.

The second event which underlined Mazumdar's high regard came when he was approached by Subhas Chandra Bose who was travelling through Nazi Germany. Bose was an Indian Nationalist leader whose aim was to deliver a British free India and he lived by slogans such as 'Give me blood, and I will give you freedom!' The Nazis supported Bose and permitted him to recruit from German prison camps to staff his Free Indian Legion whose recruits swore an oath of allegiance to the Führer and Bose himself. Not only did Bose want Mazumdar for his experience as a field medic but also to broadcast on his radio service, the Free India Centre station which broadcast a variety of anti-British propaganda to the major cities in India. Banter in the mess was high as Gris Davies-Scourfield shouted 'Goodbye Jumbo, have a good war in Burma'. Mazumdar greatly admired Bose and his aim to drive the British out of India. 'That bloody Mazumdar is a spy,' Harry Elliot was heard to mutter within earshot of the Indian doctor. He replied 'Did you call me a spy? I give you just five minutes to withdraw the accusation.' The threat of violence was not without risk, Mazumdar was a man of 5ft and 7in whilst Elliot was comfortably over 6ft and towered over the smaller man. Elliot refused to apologize and Mazumdar struck through sheer exhaustion and frustration landing a flashing cross to Elliot's jaw, sending the Guardsman to the floor. Mazumdar seized his chance and jumped on him, knees into his chest and legs holding him in place he landed furious blows until he was dragged away by onlookers.

As the Senior British Officer Colonel Stayner interviewed Mazumdar and asked for an explanation for his behaviour and insulting a senior officer. After explaining that his actions were caused by the frustration of being treated with suspicion by what should be his allies and friends, Stayner permitted Mazumdar to meet with Bose. Many officers in Colditz expected him to join the Free Indian Legion when he travelled first class to Berlin from where a chauffeur-driven Mercedes took him to the Free India Centre headquarters in the Tiergarten area of the city. Taken to Bose's private quarters, the two men had lunch whilst a pitch was made to Mazumdar. Up to this point many Indian men had joined Bose from the Allied ranks, but not a commissioned officer from the British Army, it was hoped Mazumdar would be an example to others. Bose explained how he had been a prisoner of the British and had spent 15 years fighting against rule over India. He implored Mazumdar to join him as the two men continued to talk long into the evening. Mazumdar politely refused. explaining that he too disliked British rule and hoped to gain independence for his country, but he had taken an oath of allegiance to King George VI and he could not renege. Finally, at 2.00 am Bose asked Mazumdar to consider his offer and decide over breakfast,

Over breakfast Bose wanted a direct answer, Mazumdar explained that he strongly sympathized with Bose's position as he himself opposed the British, but ultimately the answer was no, Mazumdar had taken an oath. Bose was clearly disappointed and replied, 'I have chosen my way, and you have chosen yours. Goodbye and good luck.' A servant opened the door and Mazumdar walked out after thanking Bose for his hospitality, Bose simply replied that when Mazumdar changed his mind, he would still be welcome in the Free Indian Legion. On the return journey to Colditz, which was as far from First Class as possible, Mazumdar hoped that this fresh reminder of his loyalties would endear more kindness from his fellow officers and prisoners incarcerated in the Castle. The reality was very different. Officers in Colditz were suspicious of Mazumdar for not accepting the opportunity to help gain his country's independence and why the Indian doctor had not taken the opportunity whilst outside of the Castle to escape. On returning to the British quarters the mockery began, Davies-Scourfield was particularly surprised and asked if Bose didn't want him. Mazumdar replied 'Oh yes, he wanted me very much, but I couldn't go with him could I? I have a King's commission and that is where my loyalty must lie, regardless of my personal and private feelings.' Harry Elliot was the first to apologise.

Mazumdar was unhappy at Colditz. Friendless and isolated, his religion was also not afforded the same consideration as he wished and he had not spoken to a compatriot in his mother tongue for years, he wiled away the hours alone by writing poems in Bengali. Escape was at the forefront of his mind despite his value inside the Castle as a doctor. The Senior British Officer explained to Mazumdar that the precious resources available for planned escapes would not be used to help him. At this period German civilians would have not seen an Indian national and he would have hindered any possible escape attempt. Mazumdar accepted the decision with good grace but retained a fierce determination to prove to Colonel Stayner that he would succeed. Mazumdar decided to protest about his presence in a non-Indian camp. This request was ignored as the Kommandant explained the Indian doctor was *Deutschfeindlich* and was in the correct camp. By this time a second doctor had arrived in Colditz, the Irishman Ion Ferguson. This was a significant moment as it played into Mazumdar's hands, he could be released as there was a replacement medic. News had also filtered through to the prisoners that the Nazification of prison camps had begun with several camps established in France to house Indian nationals. If Mazumdar could get transferred to such a camp escape would be much easier than in Colditz. In addition, he could converse in Bengali, get away from prejudice and mockery and hopefully, get some improved food. In conversation with Ferguson he said; 'You know, Ferguson, I have decided not to stay here any longer. There's no good an Indian trying to escape through Germany, so I shall just have to arrange to go out the main gate. I'm prepared to bet you I shall not be here in a fortnight.'

Mazumdar followed the example of Mahatma Ghandi who had begun a hunger strike, Mazumdar's would coincide with the activist. On 10 February 1943 the Indian activist was arrested and imprisoned without charge insisting he would eat nothing until he was released. On 17 February Mazumdar refused everything but salt and water. The British officers openly mocked him, shouting 'Jumbo is doing a Ghandi'. After seven days Mazumdar lost 7lbs and was fading quickly, Ferguson became concerned and asked him to stop his protest. After two weeks Mazumdar was too weak to stand, Eggers was seriously concerned and did not want the death of an Indian national on his conscience, messages flew between Berlin and Colditz. Every four hours Dr Ferguson would report to the Kommandant on the patient's health, into the third week Mazumdar's heart began to slow and his eyesight began to dwindle. Berlin was anxious that the death of an Indian national, and one Bose had attempted to recruit, would be dreadful propaganda for Hitler.

On Day 16 of the hunger strike Berlin sent word to Colditz that the Indian doctor could halt his hunger strike protest and as soon as he had regained his strength he would be permitted to leave the prison. News of his 'escape' soon flooded the Castle and Mazumdar appeared in the inner courtyard for a few moments, weak and gaunt but he acknowledged the cheers raining down from the windows, finally the officers in the prison treated him as an equal. The Escape Committee considered his escape as the start of a potential 'home run' so Dick Howe knew of his plan and gave him an arse-creeper with some German money stuffed inside. On 26 February 1943 Mazumdar walked out of the main gate at Colditz.

Initially Mazumdar spent just a week in a small camp near Bayonne in south-west France where he continued to regain his strength, he was then placed on a train heading North to which, he presumed, would be the Indian only camp. Buoyed by his arse-creeper and confident he was fit enough Mazumdar confided in fellow prisoners that he was ready to jump from the moving train as the next part of his escape. Protests from fellow passengers were waived away and he enlisted the help of two Indian sappers, who managed to pull away the bars covering a window and prized the little Indian doctor through it. The train was moving very fast and they pleaded with Mazumdar to come back inside, but before a reply was given Mazumdar had jumped! Landing on a damp field Mazumdar rolled but caught his finger in the turf which broke it. Otherwise he was remarkably intact and would fashion a splint for his finger from small branches. Planning to walk South toward neutral Spain he moved from Angoulême and relied on peasants to help him with food and warm clothing. He made good progress until a small village near Toulouse, where he was lost and unable to find a bridge to cross a deep river, asking an elderly man who offered to guide him was a crucial error. Mazumdar was 'guided' to a police station and placed under arrest.

After a few days Mazumdar was delivered to German authorities and the welcome was not warm. The escape so soon after the hunger strike was humiliating for the Germans as they had been outsmarted by the Indian doctor, the Gestapo were also well informed that he rejected the offer of Bose to help drive the British out of India. Mazumdar was beaten severely as the Gestapo demanded to know which French civilians had helped him reach Toulouse and why he had rejected the opportunity to join a German ally. After one savage beating where Mazumdar's nose would not stop bleeding the Gestapo extended the offer to join Bose again, which Mazumdar promptly refused and consequently suffered a further beating. Fearing execution, Mazumdar was relieved to be informed he would be taken to an Indian only camp at Frontstalag 153 in Chartres. He reasoned that as an Indian national the Gestapo would not kill him for fear of upsetting recruits to Bose's Free India Legion. At Frontstalag 153 he was the most senior officer but once he regained his strength Mazumdar revisited his complaints of German hospitality whilst exploring any opportunity to escape, complaining loudly that the medical supplies and food were insufficient for sick men. On one occasion he managed to saw through his cell bar windows and squeezed out and managed to scale the 20ft perimeter wall which had been laced with shards of glass before the beam of the searchlight landed on him and he surrendered. After a month and a half in solitary confinement Mazumdar was viewed as a dangerous escaper and given his own personal guard during the day. The irony was not lost on Mazumdar that his actions at Frontstalag 153 were sufficient to see him transferred back to Colditz! The guard made life very difficult for Mazumdar as he followed him everywhere, even to the toilet, which made gathering the necessary tools for an escape very challenging. After his medical duties were seen to, he was locked in a three-storey block guarded by five Algerian sentries along with other prisoners branded as troublemakers. On top of the block were machine guns and it was separated from the rest of the camp by successive belts of barbed wire. Whilst locked away in this block Mazumdar made his first real friend since capture at Neufchatel-en-Bray. Trooper Dariao Singh was a giant of a man with huge hands and a long flowing black beard, a Sikh from the Punjab and committed escaper. The two men soon hatched a plan.

On the night of 4 June 1943 the two friends broke out of the three-storey building, Singh used makeshift tools to create a small hole in a cell wall which opened out into a room where there was a window. The men silently removed the tin plates and nails which had been used to secure the window and dropped to the ground and cool night air. What lay before them was a mammoth task, the outer gate was over 500 yards away with barbed wire and fences to navigate under the glare of searchlight which Mazumdar noted made it seem like a summer's day. So they began, Singh used home-made tinsnips (manufactured from his metal bed frame) to silently cut through the barbed wire and fence which was the first obstacle, ten yards further on was another wire fence, and another. It was a clear night and when the beam of the searchlight swept in their direction the men clung flatly to the ground beneath them, and then rain came. Singh and Mazumdar were buoyed, the drizzle would create noise to mask their movement across the dusty ground and help dull the searchlights around the camp. As they finally arrived at the perimeter wall near the main gate the men drew breath and looked up at the 18ft-high barrier to freedom. Singh climbed up the wall using footholds in the broken masonry and cut through several rolls of barbed wire, he beckoned to Mazumdar who was heaved up and over the wall by the giant trooper. Gently the men climbed down the outer side of the wall and vanished into a thicket of trees, Singh whispered 'Shabash, Doctor, Shabash' (Bravo) as they set off to place distance between themselves and the camp. Mazumdar was enormously grateful for Singh's skill and strength. 'He was absolutely splendid, no words of mine can adequately express his daring, courage and perseverance.'

Neither man was equipped for a successful escape, both were still wearing their battledress (which was filthy from crawling through mud) and had just a few cigarettes between them. Singh threw his homemade tools in a pond just in case they were searched. When dawn broke the friends rested in a hedge and agreed they would travel to Switzerland by foot but only walk during the night, avoid contact with people unless absolutely necessary and take turns to rest during the day. The Swiss border was 360 miles away and three large rivers lay in their path. Singh and Mazumdar avoided walking near towns, main roads and even minor routes through the French countryside, ensuring they found remote areas to sleep during the day. After several days both of them were starving. They found a remote farm and politely knocked on the farmhouse door. The owner listened to the story of the two men and immediately took them in and provided clothes, food and wine whilst regaling the men with French hatred of Hitler and the Nazi Party. Mazumdar was moved by the bravery of the civilians who risked so much to help the pair reach neutral Switzerland.

After two weeks of walking Mazumdar and Singh were close to the Swiss border, to ensure success the men needed a guide to take them across the guarded border safely. In the foothills of Jura the men approached the frontier near Dole and found a remote farmhouse in need of urgent repair. Knocking on the door the two friends were greeted by an elderly lady who gave them a warm welcome and expressed surprise that they had managed to travel so far dressed in uniform, a testament to the skill of both men. After an excellent meal of bread and cheese washed down with some excellent red wine, the men explained their predicament. The elderly lady gave a Gallic wave of her hand and explained she could find a trustworthy guide to take the men the last few miles and ensure safe passage into neutral Switzerland. Mazumdar protested, understanding the penalties for helping escaping prisoners of war, but the elderly lady would not hear of it, stating without a guide to the lightly guarded areas the men were as good as dead. The following evening a young boy appeared to guide Mazumdar and Singh into the hills, the elderly lady waving them off. Mazumdar tried to find her identity after the war had ended but to no avail. Later that evening, after just three hours of walking the young boy pointed in the direction the men were to walk and wished them luck. At 9.00 pm on 13 July 1943 Mazumdar and Singh stumbled into the police station in the Swiss village of La Rippe.

Mazumdar enjoyed a number of months in residence at the Hotel Montreux on the shore of Lake Geneva and busied himself with treating the prisoners of war who had escaped from captivity. He even found time to begin a love affair with a Swiss woman named Elianne. Enjoying the Swiss cuisine and good wine Mazumdar settled into relative comfort and enjoyed playing billiards and bridge with his friend, Petty Officer Hammond, at the social club formed by the British. Sadly, this enjoyment did not prevail, the air of suspicion remained. The British were extremely wary of Mazumdar's contact with Subhas Chandra Bose and suspected him of spying and possibly acting as a recruiter of men for Bose's Indian nationalist army. Mazumdar was summoned to an interview with Lieutenant Colonel Henry Foote who described the doctor as '…needlessly verbose and cantankerous who displays a reluctance to talk of Bose or his visit to Berlin'.

Unknown to Mazumdar the British Government and MI5 had established a special intelligence unit named Section Z to gather information on Indian nationalism and disobedience. The Indian doctor was an innocent victim of the politics being played out against the backdrop of the Second World War. The fears of Bose and a Nationalist uprising were further ignited by Bose visiting Japan and gaining support from Emperor Hirohito's government to establish the Provisional Government for a Free India. Mazumdar began to receive rough treatment. Initially he was the subject of exclusion from the British social club for using the billiards table with a man of insufficient rank, the billiards table was not for Petty Officers. Unkind nicknames resurfaced, Jumbo and latterly 'Bengali Baboo', and Mazumdar was instructed to end his relationship with Elliane and subsequently framed for theft of British Army funds. A colonel who Mazumdar never identified engaged him at the hospital in which he worked and instructed Mazumdar to ensure that none of his countrymen would socialize with Swiss girls. Mazumdar understood this was solely directed to himself alone. Mazumdar replied politely that as long as British officers socialized with Swiss girls then he would do so as well, and the order could not be a valid one. Suspicion remained.

Some weeks later Mazumdar was drawn into a tawdry affair where the Senior British Officer in Switzerland, Lieutenant Colonel Sidney Lavender, would frame him for stealing. The treatment offered in Switzerland for British soldiers was lacking in certain areas, one such provision was eyecare. A number of troops were suffering with eye injuries or conditions and Mazumdar requested permission to order a specialised instrument called a ophthalmoscope from Geneva. Following the procedure Mazumdar obtained paperwork from the Senior Medical Officer and withdrew the money from petty cash. Lavender demanded to see Mazumdar the following day and accused him of fraud, embezzlement and in the words of the Senior British Officer, 'You're a bloody liar!'. A shocked Mazumdar was taken aback with the coarseness of Lavendar's language and explained he was not used to such abuse and disrespect, Lavendar began shouting about Indian corruption and how the Indian doctor was an example of everything wrong with India and why the nation was not fit for independence. Mazumdar, who was also on his feet and extremely angry with Lavender's behaviour, replied; 'The difference with you and me, Colonel, is you have lived in my country for twenty-five years and you can't speak one of its languages. I have lived in yours for fifteen and speak five languages, including yours.'

With that Mazumdar was arrested and taken to a hotel in Locarno to await court martial. Mazumdar had displayed only the highest regard for his commission in the British Army, rejected offers from his countrymen to fight for independence and provided excellent treatment for wounded soldiers. During his years as a prisoner of war he suffered discrimination and loneliness from the men he would call comrades, now the British Army sought to remove his name from the medical register and deny him the right to work as a doctor. Mazumdar was in despair. Eventually after nearly twenty weeks of confinement in the hotel at Locarno a representative of the intervening power paid him a visit, the Swiss colonel listened intently to Mazumdar's story, his capture and incarceration, escape from captivity and his visit to Berlin to meet Bose. Considering the treatment of Mazumdar by the British as grossly exaggerated, he moved him to a nursing home for injured soldiers and put Mazumdar to work. As one of the medics, he was transferred back to England in November 1944. Later he discovered that the staff member who had supplied the ophthalmoscope was bribed to claim that it had not been sold to Mazumdar. Despite spending many months in neutral territory, Mazumdar still had not reached freedom.

Arriving at Woolwich Barracks Mazumdar worked hard tending to the needs of wounded soldiers returning from the Normandy landings and conflict across Continental Europe, two weeks after returning to the United Kingdom he realized that he was still far from a free man. MI5 had opened a file on Mazumdar and given him a label 'Z/240' whilst they established his connections with Indian subversion. Summoned to London for an interview in the War Office, the MI5 cross-examiner asked about his contact with Bose and his trip to Berlin, Mazumdar replied in short answers and provided the minimum of detail. The file has a sentence scribbled down 'Z/240 – it seems impossible that Z/240 has forgotten as much as he pretends'. Despite the cross-examiner praising Mazumdar's loyalty he grew frustrated with the limited detail and barked 'You are ruining your chances of a medal you know'. Incredulous, Mazumdar replied, 'Do you think I escaped and went through all these things just to get a bloody medal? With that, the interview was at an end. The irony dawned on Mazumdar that he must have been the only Allied soldier of any nationality to receive better treatment in Berlin during the war than London.

On 18 August 1945 the plane carrying Subhas Chandra Bose from Taiwan to Japan ran into difficulties taking off from Taihoku Airport after refuelling, as the plane moved down the runway part of its engine dislodged from the left wing and the pilot could not control the aircraft as it lunged to the left side of the runway and burst into flames. Bose died from severe burns to his chest. With the death of Bose and the end of the Second World War, Birendra Nath Mazumdar finally found freedom many years after escaping Colditz Castle. Electing to remain in England he became a GP in Wales and settled into married life with Joan and raised two sons. In retirement the family settled in Devon until his death in December 1997 at the age of 82.

The Belgian Escape

Brigadier-General Louis Remy – Belgium

Louis Remy was born on 14 July 1918 in Brussels. A skilled linguist and sportsman, Remy played golf, tennis, squash and became a proficient skier in his teenage years, as well as fluent in Flemish, English, French and German, before turning his attention to horses prior to the outbreak of war in 1939. In 1936 Remy had joined the Belgian Air Force and trained as a pilot and observer at the Belgian Military Aviation College. Upon the outbreak of war Remy enlisted in the RAF and trained as a pilot in Canada, later as a bomber pilot, the Flight Lieutenant joined 103 Squadron RAF. The Battle for Belgium began on 10 May 1940 and ended just 18 days later. The Nazi Blitzkrieg swept through the country and forced the Allied withdrawal from continental Europe as the British Expeditionary Force escaped from Dunkirk. Remy fought bravely against overwhelming odds continuing the fight against the Nazis and was captured in August 1940, three months after the fall of France.

Whilst held in Oflag VIII-C Remy made three escape attempts and was recaptured each time. However, he gained increasingly proficient skills in forgery and on each escape he became more successful. It was believed by the camp guards that if he escaped again he might well succeed in reaching neutral Switzerland so Remy was selected to join the other 'persistent escapers' in Colditz in April 1942. Remy surveyed the surroundings at Colditz and immediately appreciated the challenges of simply setting foot outside the Castle and crossing the barrier of the Zwickauer Mulde river just below. So, Remy decided to pay a visit to the camp doctor.

Remy was in perfect health. However, he engaged the doctor in a lengthy discussion of which ailment was easiest to feign and serious enough to ensure a transfer to a hospital for an operation. Upon leaving the doctor

Remy began showcasing his talents as an actor and displayed the textbook medical symptoms of gallbladder problems. Fooling his fellow prisoners was one thing, but gaining the medical certification from the German medical officer was essential if Remy was to leave Colditz. He played his part beautifully and was soon on his way to a hospital in Schnauschwitz alongside Squadron Leader Brian Paddon and two Polish officers. Whilst in the hospital awaiting tests all four decided to flee with minimal civilian clothing, the Polish Lieutenant Just even having OFLAG IV-C imprinted on his trousers! Remy and Just reached Leipzig train station and came under suspicion of the guards who checked their hastily put-together identity papers as they sat in a train compartment. At this moment Remy decided to make a dash for it, leaving behind an overcoat he stole from the hospital, Just realized after a few minutes that Remy would not be returning and tried to leave himself but civilians pointed out that his friend had left his overcoat. Just explained it was not his but the guards heard the exchange and closed in. Just was arrested.

Remy made swift progress to Switzerland and was placed on a repatriation line through safe houses in France and Spain until he reached Algeciras, in the port of Gibraltar. Across the bay was a British ship that would provide him with safe passage to the United Kingdom. Reluctant to wait for a boat to cross the bay or a guide to help him walk the route Remy swam across the Bay of Algeciras to climb aboard the British ship. Remy was posted to Elsham Wolds in July 1944 and continued the fight for freedom against Nazi Germany in Europe between August 1944 and January 1945, ending the war as a captain with a Distinguished Flying Cross. Remy remained in the Belgian Air Force after the war and transferred his ability, intelligence, drive and determination to his role as General-Brigade Commandant of NATO at Goch. He passed away on 13 September 1992.

Colditz Today

Eighty-four years have passed since the Laufen Six, including Major Pat Reid, entered the Castle to join the Polish contingent already housed in the escape-proof Oflag IV-C. In 2006 the Castle underwent a restoration paid for by the state of Saxony which returned the walls to pre-Second World War colours. The castle is now one of the most beautiful Central German architectural monuments of the sixteenth century.

After such a turbulent history, peace and tranquillity has arrived in Colditz, the Castle is now a successful tourist destination with tours guiding guests through the most daring escapes made by prisoners during the Second World War. Part of the Castle is a youth hostel and I am pleased to say that conditions have improved immeasurably since the 1940s, with light airy guest rooms and conference facilities. Inside the Escape Museum there are exhibitions which showcase some of the homemade tools used to tunnel from inside the clocktower by the French and false papers and civilian clothing fashion by British troops. Little did Reinhold Eggers know that when he created his escape museum during the war to educate his guards that visitors would pay to see the very same items over 80 years later. The influx of visitors has helped to pay for the renovation of the chapel, which has been fully restored, and a glass flagstone covers the French tunnel.

Life before the war is also remembered in the Castle, one art exhibition remembers the eighty-four victims of 'euthanasia 'during the years the Castle acted as a mental hospital. There is also a history of the Castle during the Middle Ages and religious wars which inflicted so much damage on the building. In the spring air Colditz has a peace to it which is richly deserved.

Peter Hawthorne
March 2025

List of Escape Attempts 1941–1945

Escape Attempts in 1941

March 18 1941	Lt. B. Cazaumayou Lt. J. Paillie	French	Tunnel in the north-west tower.	Detected.
March (third week) 1941	Flt. Lt. W. Gassowski Flt. Lt. W. Gorecki	Polish	Cut bar in canteen.	Detected.
March (third week) 1941	Lt. A. Boucheron Lt. J. Charvet	French	Canteen window.	Detected.
April 5 1941	Lt. J. Just Lt. R. Bednarksi	Polish	Escaped from train en route to Konigswartha Hospital.	Recaptured in Krakow, Poland.
April 11 1941	Lt. A. Le Ray	French	Le Ray climbed up the bank from the pathway leading to the exercise yard and hid in Terrace House.	**Home run.**
April 25 1941	Lt. K. Dokurno Lt. P. Zielinski Lt. S. Bartoszewicz	Polish	Ceiling above canteen.	Detected.
May 8 1941	Lt. P. Allan	British	Escaped inside a paillasse from the prisoner of war yard as a cart loading them went out the main gate.	Recaptured in Vienna, Austria.
May 8 1941	Lt. J. Hyde-Thomson	British	Escaped inside a paillasse from the prisoner of war yard as a cart loading them went out of the main gate.	Detected.
May 9 1941	Lt. M. Chmiel Lt. M. Surmanowicz	Polish	Hid in German quarters.	Detected.
May 10 1941	Capt. P. Reid Flt. Lt. H. Wardle	British	Tunnel discovered which had begun in January 1941 – discovery in the Seam room.	Detected.

Date	Name	Nationality	Method	Result
May 11/12 1941	Lt. M. Chmiel Lt. M. Surmanowicz	Polish	The men lowered a bedsheet rope from the solitary cells from which they had sawn through the bar.	Detected.
May 13 1941	Lt. J. Just	Polish	Escaped from solitary confinement down the West face of the Castle.	Recaptured on the Rhine river.
May 17 1941	Lt. C. Moura Lt. R. Boutellier	French	Over roof of kitchen house.	Detected.
May 20 1941	Lt. J. Just	Polish	Escaped from Villingen Hospital.	Recaptured in Württemberg.
May 29 1941	Lt. Col. G. German Capt. Pat Reid Capt. K. Lockwood Capt. H. Elliott Capt. R. Barry Capt. R. Rowe Capt. J. Lados Capt. C. Lewthwaite Flt. Lt. N. Forbes Flt. Lt. H. Wardle Lt. P. Storie Pugh Lt. Z. Mikusinski	British / Polish	Canteen tunnel which was detected when the guard they bribed reported it to Reinhold Eggers who apprehended the men during escape.	Detected.
May 31 1941	Lieutenant R. Collin	French	Hid in rafters of park pavilion.	**Home run.**
June 9 1941	Lt. P. Mairesse Lebrun	French	Hid in rafters of park pavilion, dressed as a civilian.	Recaptured Grossbothen.
June 18 1941	Lt. P. Odry	French	Hid in rafters of park pavilion.	Recaptured Gross Sermuth.
June 25 1941	Lt. E. Boulé	French	Attempted to walk out disguised as a woman.	Detected.
July 1 1941	Lt. Pierre Mairesse Lebrun	French	Vaulted over the barbed wire fence in the exercise park.	**Home run.**
July 2 1941	Unidentified officers	Polish	Hole in chapel	Detected.
Mid-July 1941	Unidentified officers	French	Two-metre tunnel in the French quarters.	Detected.

Date	Name	Nationality	Method	Result
July 16 1941	Lt. J. Stepniak	Polish	Escaped from hospital	Recaptured Kraków, Poland.
July 18 1941	Lt. Tattischeff	French	Through wire from *Schützenhaus*.	Recaptured.
July 20 1941	Capt. H. Elliott Capt. J. Lados	British / Polish	Escaped through Terrace House.	Detected.
July 23 1941	Capt. J. Lados	Polish	From solitary cells down west side of castle.	Recaptured at the Swiss border.
July 28 1941	Lt. A. Thibaud Lt. R. Perrin	French	Through an air shaft into Kommandantur, then attempted to leave as civilian workers through gate.	Recaptured at Leisnig.
July 31 1941	Flt. Lt. F. Flinn Lt. P. Allen Lt. T. Elliott Lt. Cheetham Lt. Middleton Lt. Hyde-Thomson Lt. Barton Lt. Arcq Lt. Verkest Cadet Officer Karpf	British / Polish / Belgian	'Toilet Tunnel' – the men made a tunnel out of the British toilet and into the Kommandantur.	Detected.
July 1941	Unknown officers	French	Tunnel in French quarters.	Detected.
August 4 1941	Flt. Lt. D. Thom Lt. J. Boustead	British	Walked out dressed as a member of the Hitler Youth.	Detected.
August 13 1941	Capt. D. Dufour Lt. J. Smit	Dutch	Hid inside a well (manhole) in the exercise park.	Recaptured Singen.
August 14 1941	Capt. W. Lawton	British	Park walk with orderlies.	Recaptured Zschirla.
August 15 1941	Lt. Gerrit Dames	Dutch	Through hole in park wire, intended as diversion for Hans Larive and Francis Steinmetz's escape.	Detected.
August 15 1941	Lt. Hans Larive Lt. Francis Steinmetz	Dutch	Hid inside well.	**Home run.**
August 20 1941	Lt. Kroner	Polish	Escaped from Konigswartha Hospital.	**Home run.**

Date	Name	Nationality	Method	Result
August 21 1941	Lt. P. Durant	French	Park walk with orderlies.	Recaptured Colditz.
August 23 1941	Capt. Machiel van den Heuvel Capt. N. Hogerland	Dutch	Cut bars in canteen window and attempted to escape to the outer courtyard.	Detected.
August 28 1941	Lt. A. Neave	British	Walked out of the Gatehouse disguised as German officer.	Detected.
August 29 1941	Lt. R. Mascret	French	Escaped from Schneckwitz Hospital.	Recaptured in Mainz.
Mid-August 1941	Capt. P. Reid	British	Escaped through window of solitary confinement whilst in the town jail.	Detected.
September 1941	Lt. Col. G. German Sqn. Leader B. Paddon Maj. A. Anderson	British	Tunnel through kitchen basement.	Detected.
September 1941	Maj. C. Giebel Lt. Oscar Drijber	Dutch	Hid inside well.	**Home run.**
September 25 1941	Lt. A. Boucheron	French	Escaped from Zeitz Hospital, recaptured then escaped en-route to Düsseldorf prison.	**Home run.**
September 28 1941	Lt. Proutchenko Lt. Jurowski Lt. Wbcholzew	French	Through wire from *Schützenhaus*.	Recaptured at Schaffhausen.
October 6 1941	Lt. P. Storie-Pugh Unknown Dutch officer	British / Dutch	Out the cell window and across the roofs.	Detected.
October 7 1941	Lt. H. Desjobert	French	Attempted to climb park fence.	Detected.
October 7 1941	Unidentified officers	British	Tunnel in British wash house.	Detected.
October 14 1941	Lt. P. Odry Lt. Navelet	French	Escaped from the window at Elsterhorst Hospital.	**Home run.**
October 15 1941	Lt. J. Charvet Lt. P. Levy	French	Escaped from the window at Elsterhorst Hospital.	Recaptured Aachen.
October 22 1941	Lt. G. Diedler	French	Escaped from the window at Elsterhorst Hospital.	Recaptured outside hospital.

Date	Name	Nationality	Method	Result
October 1941	Undetected officers	French	Tunnel from quarters.	Detected.
November 8 1941	Lt. M. Leroy Lt. M. Lejeune Lt. Verlaye	Belgian / French	Cut wire of park fence.	Recaptured outside castle wall.
November 17 1941	Cadet Ensign J. Hageman Cadet Ensign F. Geerligs	Dutch	Disguised as members of the League of German Maidens.	Detected.
November 22 1941	Lt. G. Wardle Lt. Wojchieckowski	British / Polish	Hidden inside well at the exercise yard.	Detected and the German guards realized the ruse was working and sealed the manhole.
November 23 1941	Flt. Lt. D. Donaldson Flt. Lt. D. Thom	British	Over roof of Kellerhaus.	Detected.
November 23 1941	Capt. J. Rogers Capt. C. Lewthwaite Lt. G. Wardle Lt. A. Neave	British	Disguised as Polish orderlies.	Detected.
November 25 1941	Unidentified officers	British	Tunnel in British quarters.	Detected.
November 25 1941	Lt. M. Girot	French	Through main gate dressed as orderly.	Recaptured in Frankfurt.
November 28 1941	Giles Romilly	British	Dressed as orderly.	Detected.
December 12 1941	Lt. C. Douw van der Krap Sub Lt. Frits Kruimink	Dutch	Park under pile of leaves.	Detected in the *Appel* but the ruse of using the 'fake' prisoner Moritz, the model prisoner created by van Heuval, was exposed.

Date	Name	Nationality	Method	Result
December 15 1941	Capt. E. Steenhouwer Lt. J. Baron van Lynden	Dutch	Dressed as German officers who tried to leave through the gate to the Kommandantur.	Detected.
December 17 1941	Lt. J. Durand-Hornus Lt. J. Prot Lt. G. de Frondeville	French	Escaped into fog on trip to dentist in the town. Lt. J. Prot was killed in action on 29 January 1944 at Mount Belvedere, Italy.	**Home run.**

Escape Attempts in 1942

Date	Name	Nationality	Method	Result
January 5 1942	Lt. A. Neave Lt. A. Luteyn	British / Dutch	Under theatre the men cut a hole in the floor and dropped down into a passageway that led out of guardhouse. Dressed as German officers.	**Home run.**
January 6 1942	Lt. H Donkers Lt. J. Hyde-Thomson	Dutch / British	Under theatre the men cut a hole in the floor and dropped down into a passageway that led out of guardhouse. Dressed as German officers.	Recaptured Ulm station.
January 9 1942	Lt. de Bykowitz	French	Jumped from train to Riesa.	Detected.
January 14 1942	Flt. Lt. F. Flinn	British	British snow tunnel on canteen roof.	Detected.
January 16 1942	Lt. R. Madin Lt. J. Paille Lt. B. Cazaumayou (Original tunnellers) Many officers joined the planning for this escape.	French	The 'French Tunnel' from the clocktower.	Detected.

Date	Name	Nationality	Method	Result
January 20 1942	Capt. Dr. Le Guet Padre Jean-Jean	French	Ran away during private Sacrament of Confession.	Capt. Dr Le Guet recaptured at Frankfurt. Padre Jean-Jean recaptured at Saarbrucken.
January 20 1942	Cadet Officer C. Linck	Dutch	Linck hid inside postal service sack.	Detected.
January 21 1942	Capt P. Reid Lt. A. Orr-Ewing Lt. W. O'Hara Lt. Mackinsie Lt. J. Boustead Lt. E. Harrison	British	British snow tunnel on canteen roof.	Detected.
January 27 1942	Flt. Lt. N. Forbes	British	Digging under stage.	Detected.
February 27 1942	Capt. Gerrit Dames Capt. J. Hageman	Dutch	Dutch buttress tunnel under the terrace.	Detected.
March 2 1942	Flt. Lt. F. Flinn Cadet Officer C. Linck	British / Dutch	Escaped on way to *Schützenhaus*.	Recaptured just outside the Castle.
March 18 1942	Numerous officers	Multinational	Tunnel in sick bay	Detected.
March 20 1942	Lt. H. Desjobert Lt. A. Thibaud	French	Hid in cart of rubble.	Recaptured just outside the Castle.
April 4 1942	Flt. Lt. F. Flinn	British	Tunnel in British quarters.	Detected.
April 24 1942	Lt. P. Manheimer	French	Ran off whilst in the town with a guard.	Recaptured in the town of Colditz.
April 26 1942	Lt. W. Wychodzew Lt. J. Niestrzeba	Polish	Escaped from military hospital in Gnaschwitz.	Lt. W. Wychodzew recaptured at Singen Lt. J. Niestrzeba recaptured at Stuttgart.

Date	Name	Nationality	Method	Result
April 26 1942	Sqn. Leader B. Paddon Lt. J. Just	British / Polish	Escaped from military hospital in Gnaschwitz	Recaptured at Leipzig station.
April 26 1942	Capt. L. Rémy	Belgian	Escaped from train station, took boat to Algeciras.	**Home run.**
April 1942	Lt. J. Baron van Lynden	Dutch	Broke into German quarters to steal uniform.	Detected.
April 1942	Unidentified Dutch officer	Dutch	Hid in pile of leaves in park.	Detected.
May 10 1942	Lt. D. Gill and an unidentified Polish officer	British / Polish	Through the kitchen.	Detected.
May 28 1942	Lt. M. Girot	French	Replaced French orderly on working party. Lt. M Girot was killed in action by the Gestapo in May 1944.	Recaptured in Frankfurt.
May 28 1942	Lt. I. Price	British	Lt. Price exchanged places with Lt Fleury who was leaving the Castle.	Detected.
June 2 1942	Lt. M. Sinclair	British	Escaped from Leipzig Hospital.	Recaptured in Cologne.
June 8 1942	Lt. M. Sinclair	British	Escaped from holding cell.	Recaptured in Cologne.
June 9 1942	Capt. W. Lawton Capt. R. Howe Lt. W. O'Hara Lt. E. Harrison Lt. I. Dickinson Lt. V. Parker	British	In attic above British quarters.	Detected.
June 11 1942	Sqn. Leader B Paddon	British	Sent for court martial at Thorn, escaped from work party there. Smuggled out through Gdansk.	**Home run.**
June 45 1942	Lt. R. Bouillez	French	Sent for court martial in Stuttgart, jumped train but found unconscious next to tracks, sent to hospital, escaped from hospital.	**Home run.**

Date	Name	Nationality	Method	Result
July 6 1942	Unidentified Dutch Officer	Dutch	Dutch tunnel.	Detected.
July 7 1942	Lt. J. Tucki	Polish	In Polish orderly working party.	Detected.
July 15 1942	Flt. Lt. V. Parker Lt. M. Keillar	British	Flt. Lt Parker attempted to exchange places with Sgt. Gollan in a working party. Lt. M. Keillar attempted to exchange places with Sgt. Corp. Hendren in a working party. Transferred to Lamsdorf prison.	Detected.
July 19 1942	Unidentified Polish and Belgian officers	Polish / Belgian	Tunnel in Saalhaus.	Detected.
July 26 1942	Capt. Van den Heuvel Lt. H. Vinkinbosch Lt. Verleye Lt. F Kruimink Lt. P. Stoie-Pugh	Belgian / British / Dutch	Seam tunnel in the scullery.	Detected.
July 26 1942	Unidentified British officers	British	Tunnel in senior officers' quarters.	Detected.
August 18 1942	Flt. Lt. J. Dickinson	British	Jumped wall of exercise yard of Colditz town jail, stole bicycle.	Recaptured in Chemnitz.
August 19 1942	Capt. P Reid Capt. R. Barry	British	Delousing shed tunnel.	Detected.
August 20 1942	Lt. Delarne	French	Park walk disguised as painter.	Detected.
August 25 1942	Flt. Lt. N. Forbes Lt. K. Lee	British	Escaped en-route to Leipzig for court martial.	Recaptured in Leipzig.
August 28 1942	Flt. Lt. J. Dickinson	British	Hid underneath bread delivery van.	Detected.
August 29 1942	Capt. R. Barry Capt. P Reid	British	Solitary confinement: Barry cut through bars, Reid dug tunnel.	Detected.
September 1 1942	Lt. W. Zelaźniewicz	Polish	Escaped on park walk.	Recaptured in Podelwitz.

Date	Name	Nationality	Method	Result
September 2 1942	Lt. Cdr. W. Stephens	British	Escaped from Colditz train station (returning from Lamsdorf).	Recaptured outside the Castle.
September 7 1942	Flt. L. D. Bruce	British	Bruce hid inside Red Cross tea chest which was placed in the Kommandantur building, he climbed down outer wall via bedsheet rope.	Recaptured in Gdansk.
September 8 1942	Flt. Lt. J. Dickinson	British	Attempted escape while on exercise in the park.	Detected.
September 9 1942	Capt. W. Lawton Capt. T. Beets Lt. Donkers Lt. G. Wardle	British / Dutch	Broke into Kommandant's office, cut hole into storeroom, out of storeroom in German and Polish orderly uniforms.	Lt. Donkers and Lt. G. Wardle were recaptured at Commichau. Capt. W. Lawton and Capt. E. Beets recaptured at Dobeln.
September 9 1942	Flt. Lt H. Fowler Major D. van Doorninck	British / Dutch	Broke into Kommandant's office, cut hole into storeroom, out of storeroom in German and Polish orderly uniforms. Flt. Lt. H. Fowler died March 1944.	**Home run.**
September 10 1942	Unidentified British officers	British	Subaltern's tunnel	Detected
October 14 1942	Major R.B. Littledale Lt. Cdr. W. Stephens Capt. P. Reid Flt. Lt. H. Wardle	British	Escape through kitchen into German yard, across yard into Kommandantur cellar, out cellar into dry moat. Major R.B. Littledale was killed in action in August 1944.	**Home run.**

Date	Name	Nationality	Method	Result
October 23 1942	Unidentified Dutch officers	Dutch	Attempt at hole under theatre.	Detected.
October 1942	Lt. P. Storie-Pugh Lt. F. Kruimink	British / Dutch	Over roof of Kellerhaus. Discovered by a guard dog whilst hiding on the ground.	Detected.
November 26 1942	Lt. M. Sinclair Lt. C. Klein	British / French	Through the light well into the Kommandantur.	Lt. M. Sinclair was recaptured at Tuttlingen. Lt. C. Klein was recaptured at Plauen.
November 27 1942	Capt. R. Barry Lt. Aulard	British / French	Through the light well into the Kommandantur.	Detected.
November 1942	Lt. M. Bissell	British	Tunnel under altar steps in chapel.	Detected.
December 6 1942	Lt. Z. Kepa Lt. T. Osiecki Lt. A. Slipko	Polish	Over orderlies' roof.	Detected.
December 14 1942	Lt. M. Sinclair	British	From Weinsberg after recapture – Lt. Sinclair escaped custody but was rearrested.	Recaptured in Weinsberg.
December 15 1942	Lt. van der Falk Bouman	Dutch	Disguised as German soldier	Recaptured in Emmendingen.
December 19 1942	E.R.A (Engine Room Artificer) W. Hammond. E.R.A D. Lister	British	E.R.A Hammond and Lister claimed they were not in the right camp as they were not officers. Transferred to Lamsdorf since not officers, escaped from Breslau work party.	Both would escape captivity and reach Switzerland.
December 28 1942	Lt. A. Perodeau	French	Impersonated Willi Pöhnert.	Detected.

Escape Attempts 1943

Date	Name	Nationality	Method	Result
January 1943	Lt. Gris Scourfield-Davies Others	British	Pulpit tunnel under chapel.	Detected.
March 7 1943	Capt. B. Mazumdar	British (India)	Mazumdar went on hunger strike in order to receive a transfer to an Indian only camp. Mazumdar eventually escaped to Switzerland.	**Home run.**
March 7 1943	Flt. Lt. J. Dickinson	British	Jumped over wall of exercise area of Colditz town jail.	Recaptured in Chemnitz.
April 5 1943	Capt. D. Dufour Flt. Lt. A. van Rood	British / Dutch	Dressed as German officers.	Detected.
April 8 1943	Capt. Pemberton-How	British	*Schützenhaus*. In manhole after search.	Detected.
April 8 1943	Lt. E. Desbats Lt. J. Caillaud	French	Over roof of Castle.	Detected.
April 28 1943	Capt. Dr. I Ferguson RAMC	British	Capt. Dr. Ferguson wrote a letter to his friend, the son of the Irish Prime Minister asking Ireland to join the war. Transferred to another camp shortly afterwards. Capt. Dr. Ferguson worked as doctor at Stalag IV-D certifying prisoners insane. Convinces Germans he is himself insane, repatriated in January 1945.	Insanity.
April 1943	Undetected British Officers	British	Hole under dentist office chair.	Detected.
May 1 1943	Flt. Lt. V. Parker Flt. Lt. N. Forbes Lt. D. Wheeler	British	'Revier' tunnel.	Detected.
May 11 1943	Flt. Lt. D. Thom	British	Flt. Lt. Thom vaulted he wire fence of the park.	Recaptured outside wall.
May 1943	Lt. M. Sinclair Lt. G. Davies-Scourfield	British	Cut hole in park fence wire.	Detected.

Date	Name	Nationality	Method	Result
May 1943	Flt. Lt. J. Best Lt. M. Harvey and other British officers who remained undetected.	British	Attempted to re-open 'French Tunnel'.	Detected.
June 7 1943	Lt. J.J.L. Baron van Lynden	Dutch	During Dutch transfer to Stanislau.	Not regarded as a Home Run as the whole Dutch contingent were transferred to Stanislau.
June 11 1943	Lt. A. Perrin	French	Through 'witches' walk'.	Detected.
July 8 1943	Lt. M. Fahy	French	Escaped from the hospital in Hohentein-Ernstthal.	Recaptured in Kaufungen.
July 12 1943	Lt. A. Darthenay	French	Escaped from hospital in Hohentein-Ernstthal. Joined French Resistance. Lt. A. Darthenay was killed in action by the Gestapo on 7 April 1944.	**Home run.**
July 13 1943	Lt. C. Klein Giles Romilly	Free French/ British	Hidden in baggage pile at Colditz rail station.	Detected.
July 13 1943	Lt. T. Barrott Lt. D. Hamilton Lt. C. Sandbach	British	Exchanged identities with French officers in transit to Lubeck.	Detected.
July 1943	Lt. J. Best Lt. M. Harvey Others	British	'French Tunnel' re-opening attempt.	Detected.
August 10 1943	Lt. P. Allan Lt. A. Campbell and other British officers who remained undetected.	British	'Whitechapel Deep' tunnel.	Detected.
September 3 1943	Capt. L. Pope Lt. M. Sinclair Lt. J. Hyde-Thomson	British	'Franz Josef' escape.	Detected.
September 11 1943	Lt. W. Miller Lt. R. Boustead	British	Exchanged places with Lt. Stepninc and Lt. Jablonowski during Polish transfer.	Detected.

Date	Name	Nationality	Method	Result
September 16 1943	Lt. A. Orr-Ewing	British	As French orderly on exercise.	Detected.
September 30 1943	Lt. G. Davies-Scourfield	British	Lt. G. Scourfield-Davies escaped out of the prisoner's yard in a rubbish cart dressed as a Gefrieter and left the Castle via the park. Lt. Scourfield-Davies place at *Appel* was taken by a ghost (a prisoner who hid, feigning escape, in the Castle and reappeared at *Appel* to make it appear no officer had escaped).	Recaptured in Hildescheim.
September 1943	Unidentified British officers	British	'Mayfair Maggies' tunnel in the room next to the dentist's surgery. (No doubt hoping the dentist's drilling would cover the noise of their digging!)	Detected.
October 7 1943	Lt. A. Orr-Ewing	British	The same escape method as Lt. G. Scourfield-Davies.	Detected.
November 3 1943	Cpl. Green Cpl. Fleet	British	Orderlies who escaped from work party at Colditz train station.	Recaptured in Cottbus.
November 25 1943	Lt. J. Rawson	British	Lt. Rawson exchanged places with Cpl. Aitken on a party to Muhlberg.	Detected.

Escape Attempts 1944

Date	Name	Nationality	Method	Result
January 19 1944	Lt. M. Sinclair Lt. J. Best	British	Sixty-second rope escape down west terrace	Recaptured in the Rheine.
January 28 1944	Lt. W. Millar	Canadian	Broke into German courtyard, hung from bottom of German truck as it left the Castle. Believed killed by SS at Mauthausen in July 1944.	**Home run** – it is thought that Lt. W. Millar reached a safe house in Czechoslovakia but was arrested in that safe house by the Gestapo and shot.
January 31 1944	Capt. C. Lewthwaite	British	Hid under a rubbish pile in the park.	Detected

Date	Name	Nationality	Method	Result
February 3 1944	Lt. A. Orr-Ewing	British	Jumps a fence in the exercise park, swims across Mulde river.	Recaptured in the town.
March 17 1944	British Naval officers – unidentified.	British	'Crown Deep' tunnel in the Kellerhaus.	Detected.
March 26 1944	Flt. Lt. V. Parker Lt. M. Harvey	British	From air-raid shelter in the cellar the men escaped down a cobbled alley to the outer permitter.	Detected. 'Ghosts' who replaced Flt. Lt. Parker and Harvey were also detected.
April 19 1944	Flt. Lt. D. Bruce	British	Cut bars on north side of castle, reached wire fence before being detained.	Detected.
April 29 1944	Lt. D. Moir Lt. M. Edwards Lt. D. Wheeler Lt. P. Fergusson	British	Intentionally sloppy escape. The men cut through the seam in the Kommandantur in an attempt to be placed in town jail.	Detected – the men decided to abandon the escape from the town jail after hearing about the successful D-Day landings.
April 1944	Two unidentified British officers	British	*Hexengang* corridor.	Detected.
April 1944	Lt. J. Hamilton-Baillie	British	Into sewers through shower drain.	Detected.
May 2 1944	Lt. J. Beaumont	British	Hidden under blanket sown with leaves in the park.	Recaptured about 2 miles from Colditz.
May 3 1944	Lt. G. Wardle	British	Escape through orderlies quarters	Detected.
May 5 1944	Capt. H. Elliott Flt. Lt. F. Flinn Lt. J. Barnett Lt. M. Wynn	British	Faked illnesses and successfully 'worked their ticket'. Repatriated by the Medical Commission. Capt. Elliot – Stomach Ulcer Flt. Lt Flynn – Madness Lt. J. Barnett – High blood pressure Lt. M. Wynn – Back injury as a result of wounds at the St Nazaire Raid.	**Home run.**
May 29 1944	Capt. F. Weldon Lt. J. Hamilton-Baillie	British	Out of POW yard into Kommandantur attics, into storeroom on south side of German yard.	Detected.

Date	Name	Nationality	Method	Result
June 1 1944	Maj. A. Anderson Others	British	'Dentist chair' tunnel.	Detected.
June 13 1944	Lt. L. Pumphrey Lt. M. Riviere	British	Tunnel through British kitchens.	Detected.
June 16 1944	Maj. R. Lorraine Flt. Lt. D. Bruce 'Bosun' J. Chrisp	British	Tunnel through sewers into German yard.	Detected.
July 14 1944	Flt. Lt. D. Thom	British	Escaped from hospital at Schmorkau.	Recaptured.
September 4 1944	Lt. M. Sinclair	British	Jumped fence in park, wearing civilian clothes.	Detected.
September 18 1944	Capt. C. Lewthwaite	British	Park walk under pile of leaves.	Detected.
September 25 1944	Lt. M. Sinclair	British	Jumped over fence wire in park.	Shot dead.
From September 1 1945 until April 15 1945	Flt. Lt. W. Goldfinch Flt. Lt. J. Best Lt. A. Rolt Lt. G. Wardle Others	British	The 'Colditz Cock' glider was assembled in the attic above the chapel and would be propelled out of the attic by a bathtub filled with rubble. A prisoner would land in nearby fields across the river and escape on foot. By the end of the war the glider was complete but the runway (wooden runners were still under construction).	Unused (prison liberated by Allied forces prior to completion of glider).

Escape Attempts 1945

Date	Name	Nationality	Method	Result
April 1945	Lt.Col. M.B. Reid	British	The oldest British prisoner. Feigned heart disease by smoking heavily and drinking concentrated black coffee prior to medical examination and was repatriated.	Home run.

Appendix 2

Staff List of Colditz Castle

Kommandants
Colonel Schmidt (1866–1946 or 1947)
Commandant of Colditz, October 1939–31 July 1942
Colonel Glaesche (1889–1968)
Commandant of Colditz, August 1942–13 February 1943
Lieut. Colonel Prawitt (1899–1969)
Commandant of Colditz, 13 February 1943–15 April 1945

Second-in-Command
Major Menz, 2-I-C, 1939–August 1941
Lieutenant Colonel von Kirchbach, 2-I-C, August 1941–February 1942
Captain Paul Priem, 2-I-C, February 1942–13t October 1942
Colonel Kalivius, 2-I-C, 13 October 1942–May 1943
Major Amthor, 2-I-C, May 1943 – February 1945
Major Howe, 2-I-C, February 1945–16 April 1945

Security Officers
Captain Hans Lange, SO, 1939 – October 1943
Major Horn, SO, October 1943–February 1944
Captain Reinhold Eggers, SO, February 1944–16th April 1945
LO1 Hauptmann Paul Priem (Duty Officer)
LO2 Rittmeister Aurich
Captain Hans Pupke, Camp Officer, 11 March 1941–16 April 1945

Bibliography

Cheshire County Memorial Project 2024 Lieutenant Colonel Ronald Bolton LITTLEDALE (cheshireroll.co.uk).

With research assistance by the Canadian Military Engineer Museum.

Baybutt, Ron, *Colditz: The Great Escapes* (Little, Brown and Company: USA, 1982).

Champ, J. and C. Burgess, *The Diggers of Colditz* (Taylor-Type Publications: Hong Kong, 1985).

Chancellor, H., *Colditz – The Definitive History* (Hodder and Stoughton: UK, 2002).

Clay, P., *Voices of Colditz* (Fonthill: Great Britain, 2014).

Davies-Scourfield, G., *In the Presence of my Foes* (Pen and Sword: Barnsley, 1991).

De Gmeline, P., 'L'as des as brittaniques: le Group Captain Douglas Bader', *39–45 Magazine* (Editions Heimdal ed., 1987), pp. 4, 5.

Dockrill, M., *Atlas of the Twentieth Century* (Ilex: Glasgow, 1991).

Duggan, M., *Padre in Colditz* (Hodder and Stoughton: UK, 1978).

Duke, F., *Name, Rank and Serial Number* (Merideth Press: London, 1969).

Eggers, R., *Colditz – The German Story* (Pen and Sword: Barnsley, 2011).

Hoskins, T., *Flight from Colditz* (Pen and Sword: Barnsley, 2016).

Jackson, R., *When Freedom Calls; Great Escapes of the Second World War* (Endeavour: London, 1973).

Larive, H., *The Man Who Came in from the Cold* (Hale Press: London, 1975).

Le Ray, A., *Première à Colditz* (Editions Arthaud: Paris, 1980).

MacKenzie, S.P., *The Colditz Myth* (Oxford University Press: Oxford, 2008).

McMally, M., *Colditz: Oflag IV-C* (Osprey Publishing: Oxford, 2010).

Neave, A., *They Have Their Exits* (Hodder and Stoughton: UK, 1953).

Pardoe, P., *From Calais to Colditz* (Pen and Sword: Yorkshire, 2016).

Reid, M., *Into Colditz* (Michael Russell Publishing: Norfolk, 1983).

Reid, P., *Colditz: The Full Story* (Macmillan: London, 1984).

Reid, P., *Escape from Colditz* (Berkeley Publishing: USA, 1952).

Reid, P., *The Colditz Story* (MacMillan: London, 1952).

Reid, P., *The Latter Days at Colditz* (Hodder and Stoughton: London, 2014).

Rogers, J., *Tunnelling into Colditz: a Mining Engineer in Captivity* (Robert Hale Ltd: London 1986).

Routledge, P., *Public Servant Secret Agent – The Elusive Life and Violent Death of Airey Neave* (Fourth Estate: UK, 2002).

Turner, J., *Douglas Bader* (Pen and Sword: Barnsley, 2009).

Walters, G., *The Colditz Legacy* (Magna Large Print Books: London, 2006).

Wood, J., *Detour* (Falcon Press: UK, 1946).

Articles
David, R., 'The education of British prisoners of war in German captivity, 1939-45', *History of Education*, 18:3 (1989), pp. 257–65
No. 218 (Gold Coast) Squadron 1936-1945 *'In-Time'* London Gazette, 6 January 1948>

Obituaries
Billie Stephens B. Rowland, Max Arthur Sunday 17 August 1997 23:02 BS

Oral Histories
Micky Wynn (Lord Newborough) 9721/3 Imperial War Museum Sound Archive.
Biren Mazumdar 4945/2. The only Indian prisoner inside Colditz, as medical officer he waited until a replacement medic was installed at Colditz and then began a hunger strike and was moved to an Indian only camp – from which he escaped to Switzerland in 1944.

Primary Materials
The King's Royal Rifle Corps Association. The National Archives.
Kees Koenen Escape from Colditz, No.218 Squadrons 'Home-Run' | No. 218 (Gold Coast) Squadron 1936-1945. Imperial War Museum Lambeth – The papers of Lt. Col. M.E. Reid 4275.

Websites
Academickids.com/Medals of England/Hedley Fowler
https://www.latimes.com/archives/la-xpm-2007-jun-08-me-leray8-story.html
https://colditzcastletours.com/colditz-ww2-pow-camp/colditz-german-jailers/
https://218squadron.wordpress.com/escape-from-colditz/
www.acre.com website – his report of pre Colditz and escape
https://www.tracesofwar.com/persons/73869/Doorninck-van-Damiaen-Joan.htm
https://www.northlincsweb.net/103Sqn/html/louis_remy_103_sqn.html David Fell
WWW.northlinksweb/netlouisremy
Max Arthur – https://www.independent.co.uk/arts-entertainment/obituary-lord-newborough-1181076.html
https://rhug.co.uk/all-news/the-war-and-lord-michael-micky-vaughan-wynne
https://www.annales.org/archives/x/frondeville.html
https://www.telegraph.co.uk/news/obituaries/1556304/General-Alain-Le-Ray.html
Escape Line
Jewishvirtuallibrary.org/Jewish-pow-s-at-colditz-castle
Hank Wardle's Escape Report (Ref WO208/3311)
Adlermilitaria.com

Index